SIR FRANCIS THROCKMORTON

(*See p. vi*)

A SEVENTEENTH CENTURY COUNTRY GENTLEMAN

(Sir Francis Throckmorton, 1640-80)

BY

E. A. B. BARNARD
M.A., F.S.A., F.R.Hist.S.

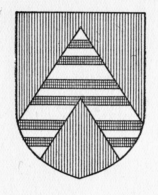

Cambridge
W. HEFFER & SONS LTD.

FIRST EDITION - - - - 1944
SECOND EDITION - . - 1948

NOTE TO SECOND EDITION

Since this book was originally published, in December, 1944, Coughton Court has become the first settled or entailed historic mansion to be acquired for the nation under the National Trust Act, 1939.

April, 1947.

Printed in Great Britain at the Works of
W. HEFFER AND SONS LTD., CAMBRIDGE, ENGLAND

Introduction

One day late in August, 1938, I happened to read an interesting report in the *Birmingham Post* concerning a visit to Coughton Court, Warwickshire—for several centuries the home of the Throckmortons—which had lately been made by the Paleographical Section of the Summer School of Librarianship, at that time meeting in Birmingham.

In the course of this report there was reference to a small 17th Century parchment-bound ledger sedulously kept by the steward of young Sir Francis Throckmorton between the years 1651 and 1660, which, together with other documents of particular paleographical or historical interest. had been selected from the Throckmorton MSS. and placed on view for the benefit of the visitors. This little exhibition had been arranged by Lady Throckmorton—now, since 1942, the Dowager Lady—who for a long time past has taken a deep interest in the family archives, and who on this occasion had the skilled assistance of Miss E. S. Scroggs.

Although I have also had some association, certainly rather superficial, with the Throckmorton MSS., I could not call to mind the ledger in question, and therefore on the next occasion that I was at Coughton Court, in February, 1939, I asked Lady Throckmorton if I might be allowed to see it. The little volume was soon forthcoming, and I quickly found that the accounts, representative of a class of document in which I have always been particularly interested, were quite new to me. Indeed, they presented distinct possibilities of elaboration, if only on account of their many mid-Commonwealth Cambridge items.

Eventually, thanks to the kindness of Sir Robert Throckmorton, the owner of the MSS., and to Lady Throckmorton, I was able to make a prolonged examination of the accounts, and then realized that not only was Cambridge well represented therein, but that there were Oxford, London, and a number of other interests also to be fully considered. Then came the idea to attempt some reconstruction of the life of young Sir Francis during the whole period covered by the accounts, and afterwards, as far as possible, to continue the story through the succeeding years until his death in 1680, when he was only in his fortieth year.

The first stage in this attempt was submitted to many members and friends of the Cambridge Antiquarian Society, in October, 1939, the title of my paper being "A Young Country Gentleman at Cambridge, 1654–57". As time went on other papers, on a wider basis, were read before the Oxford Architectural and Historical Society, the British Archaeological Association, and the Worcestershire Archaeological Society. These papers had a very encouraging reception, several speakers expressing their hope that more would ultimately be heard of Sir Francis in book-form.

At last I decided definitely to embark upon this complex undertaking, and to try to weave into a useful and carefully exact story all the many items which I saw before me, an undertaking which I realized would mean much research and movement under many adverse circumstances, the present times being especially considered. The Vale of Evesham, with Coughton Court not far distant therefrom, was my homeland, and very well-known to me, but Weston Underwood and the Buckinghamshire-Northamptonshire district were much less familiar, and closer acquaintance had to be made with them.

My undertaking has now at last been completed, and I trust that this story may prove of interest, and of some little use, particularly to students of local history, whom I have constantly had in mind during its course. I have for a long time felt that it is far better to deal with old accounts in narrative form, whenever possible, than to print many pages of items from them, which as such often possess so very little "life".

The accounts consist of 3,552 items, totalling £2,279 14s. During their course altogether some 250 people are mentioned, most of them being Roman Catholic friends of Sir Francis, and many of them connected by marriage, and 75 towns and villages are named. Many of the items are here worded as they actually appear in the accounts, but the use of parentheses to denote them has been purposely avoided except in a few necessary instances. A few of the items may seem trivial and sometimes superfluous, but they have all been included with intention. Many have been omitted, as referring to the common things of everyday life then as now, and all the items of horsey affairs—and they are somewhat numerous—have been more or less set aside. Nothing has been invented and if, as is of course quite possible,

despite great care, I have at times erred in the actual move-
ments of those with whom I have chiefly dealt, no harm
will have been done to the actual fabric of the story.

No reference has been made to the value of money during
the period covered by these accounts. There is such a
diversity of opinion upon this point that it seems wiser to
leave it alone, particularly as, in this case, it does not much
matter one way or the other. The decision must be left to
the reader.

It will be noted that young Sir Francis was somewhat
slow to put away childish things, but later, when he did so,
his life became very much that of the ordinary young man
of—well, one cannot say of to-day, when everything is so
temporarily changed, so it must be the life of the young man
of yesterday. *Plus ça change, plus c'est la même chose*, which
reminds me that William Cowper, writing indeed from his
beloved Weston Underwood at the close of the 18th Century,
said:—

"The inside of the man has, at least, undergone no change.
His passion, appetites and aims are just the same as they
ever were. Men wear perhaps a more handsome disguise
than they did in days of yore; for philosophy and literature
will have their effect upon the exterior; but in every other
respect a modern is only an ancient in a different dress".

In conclusion, perhaps a little more should be said concerning the old mansion at Weston Underwood, which often
comes into this story. Amongst other references to it may
be noted that of the late Thomas Wright, the antiquary to
whom the Olney district is so particularly indebted. In his
Tours of Cowper (Chap. XV, Weston Underwood), published
in 1893, he says:—

"Weston Hall, the ancient mansion of the Throckmoonsrt
. . . was entirely demolished in 1827; and of its near
appurtenances none are now standing except the iron gates
with four stone piers and a portion of the stabling and
granary crowned by a cupola. . . . The north, principal, or
Queen Anne front faced the park, and was built by Sir
Robert Throckmorton about 1710. . . . From the general
appearance of the interior it was judged that the house must
have been commenced about the end of the fifteenth

century; at the time of its demolition the southern portion was in ruins and had not been inhabited for 200 years. . . .

"In taking the house down several interesting discoveries were made. [These included a secret hiding-place for a priest; and a leathern purse containing twenty-eight guineas and four half-guineas of the reigns of Charles II and James II.] . . .

"The library, the family portraits, and the coats-of-arms on painted glass, with which the windows were adorned, were removed to Coughton Court, the principal residence of the family. . . ."

There is a detailed reference to the later and existing mansion in *Buckinghamshire* (Vol. II, pp. 216–18), published by the Royal Commission on Historical Monuments in 1913.

The frontispiece is reproduced, by permission of the Director and Secretary, Victoria and Albert Museum, from a portrait of Sir Francis made by Gerard Zoest (*fl.* 1637–81), still at Coughton Court. The portrait was exhibited at the National Portrait Exhibition in 1866. "The Tower of London, *c.* 1695", facing p. 17, is from the Pepysian Collection, Magdalene College, Cambridge, and is reproduced by permission of the Master and Fellows, and that of the Editors of the Wren's Society's Vol. XVIII, in which volume the illustration appeared.

During the course of these researches it has been necessary to consult a number of friends and correspondents whom I cordially thank for their always ready assistance. In this respect I am particularly grateful to Mr H. C. Andrews, F.S.A. (Hertford), Mr A. T. Bolton, F.S.A., Mr H. M. Cashmore (City Librarian, Birmingham), Canon C. W. F. Jebb (Graveley), Miss E. S. Scroggs, Miss Ethel Stokes (British Records Association), Rev. D. K. Sylvester (Fladbury and Throckmorton), the Dowager Lady Throckmorton, and Mrs Thomas Wright (Olney). Miss Jebb (Graveley) kindly photographed the ruins of Chisfield Church, but their present condition (see p. 78) conveys but little idea of the structure, and the photograph has therefore not been reproduced here.

E. A. B. BARNARD.

ST. CATHARINE'S COLLEGE,
CAMBRIDGE.

Contents

Illustrations

COUGHTON COURT IN 1829

WESTON UNDERWOOD HOUSE IN 1829

(From drawings by J. P. Neale (1780–1847))

Chapter I

EARLY YEARS, 1651–54

Francis Throckmorton, our young country gentleman who throughout these pages shall as a rule appear simply as Francis, was born at Great Coughton—at the ancestral mansion, since known as Coughton Court, near Alcester, Warwickshire, and close to the Worcestershire border—on September 13th, 1640. On January 16th, 1650–1, on the death of his father—Sir Robert—a few months after the decisive Battle of Worcester (September 3rd, 1651), he succeeded to the baronetcy which had been conferred by Charles I on his father on September 1st, 1642. His mother[1] was Sir Robert's second wife,[2] Mary, daughter of Sir Francis Smith of Ashby Folville, co. Leicester, and sister of Sir Charles Smith, later—in 1643—created first Lord Carington of Wootton Wawen, not many miles from Coughton Court. Thus the boy, born in a critical year of the troubled reign of Charles I, now became head of an old and well-known family,[3] most of whom still—despite those times—all remained unswervingly Roman Catholic,[4] and accordingly suffered heavy fines and many disabilities.

On August 22nd, 1642, the King had set up his standard at Nottingham, and some two months later—on October 23rd—the indecisive battle of Edgehill, during which Francis's uncle, Sir John Smith,[5] redeemed the royal standard, was fought not many miles from the estates of the Throckmortons in Warwickshire and Worcestershire. Francis, brought up in such fervent Royalist circles, spent

[1] She eventually married again, her second husband being Lewis Mordaunt, one of the Mordaunts of Walton Hall, Warwickshire.

[2] His first wife was Dorothy, daughter of Sir Francis Fortescue, of Salden, Bucks. She died childless in 1617, and was buried at Coughton.

[3] For pedigree see G. Lipscomb's *Buckinghamshire*, (1847), Vol. IV, pp. 399–402.

[4] It is computed that this time there were 20,000 Roman Catholics in England and Wales, which then had a population amounting to about 4,000,000.

[5] See p. 44.

his early boyhood at Coughton Court, where as time went on he must have heard much talk concerning the great events of those years, and particularly of the execution, on January 30th, 1649-50, of the hapless King to whose service his father had been so actively attached, until he was obliged to leave the mansion—plundered and occupied by Parliamentary troops—and seek refuge at Worcester. Much damage was done to the mansion at that time, and it must have given great pleasure to Francis in later years to put it into proper condition again, and to effect considerable alterations there.

The boy would certainly also hear exciting tales—less recent tales—of Guy Fawkes, of his Gunpowder Plot in 1605, and of the part which Coughton Court had then played, but with which none of the Throckmortons had been actually associated. For Sir Everard Digby had rented the mansion from the then owner, Sir Thomas Throckmorton, and here on that famous November 5th, Lady Digby and other ladies, together with the Jesuit Fathers, Garnet and Tesimond, anxiously awaited news of the Plot, of which the complete failure—initiated by Francis Tresham's betraying letter—was brought to them in the depth of the night by Thomas Bates, who had galloped over from John Grant's house at Norbrook, some ten miles distant, near Stratford-upon-Avon.

His youthful eyes must have wondered too, as he rambled about his ancestral home, and peered into its priest's hiding-places, for there must have been more than one such hiding-place at Coughton Court, although it could not have been so amply provided in that respect as was Harvington Hall,[1] over the Worcestershire border, near Chaddesley Corbett, and not many miles away. He may have known that romantic old house too, but it did not actually come into his family until his own son, Robert, the 3rd baronet, married Mary, daughter and heiress of Sir Charles Yate, through whom both Harvington Hall, and Buckland[2] in Berkshire, accrued to the Throckmortons in 1690.

---

[1] *Studies in Worcestershire History*, by John Humphreys, edited, with appendices, by E. A. B. Barnard, (Chapter V).
[2] Harvington Hall was sold in 1923, and Buckland in 1910.

As to 16th Century times, Francis must have been told
on the one hand of that other Francis (1554-84), his unfortunate ancestor, a student of the Inner Temple, whose religious
and political zeal had brought him to the Tower, and to
execution at Tyburn; and on the other of Job, that zealot's
cousin, the Puritan controversialist whose activities got
him also into trouble about the same time.

Then, too, there was Sir Nicholas, that sturdy Protestant
and very active diplomatist, who, amongst many other
experiences, was for some time confined in the Tower, also
in 1584, on suspicion of being implicated in Sir Thomas
Wyatt's Rebellion, and is erroneously said to have been
poisoned by Dudley, Earl of Leicester, Elizabeth's favourite.
This Sir Nicholas Throckmorton, who had been Chief Butler
of England, and a Chamberlain of the Exchequer, was
buried in the former church of St Katherine Cree. His
monument—removed therefrom, so it is recorded, after
the Great Fire of 1666—is still preserved in the present
church of St Katherine Cree, in the City, not far from
Throgmorton[1] Avenue and Throgmorton Street, thorough-
fares now for many years spelt thus, and bearing a name
destined, through them to become known to-day in all parts
of the world. Within this area the Throckmortons for many
years possessed property and a town house.

Going back to still earlier times, Francis would have
been shewn the finely incised brass[2] still in Fladbury Church
—not far from the South Worcestershire village of Throckmorton, one of the manors of the family, lying off the main
road about halfway between Pershore and Evesham[3]—of
the armoured John Throckmorton, Under-Treasurer of
England, who died in 1445, and Eleanor, his wife. Again,
at Coughton Church, some 15 miles from Fladbury, and
only a few yards from his own birthplace, he would look
upon those impressive 16th century memorials of other
members of his family which are still there, together with

---

[1] A form of spelling never at any time used by the family.
[2] *Trans.* Worcs. Arch. Soc., Vol. IV, pp. 34-42, with illustrations.
[3] The sites of ruined Benedictine abbeys, with both of which
various Throckmortons had been associated, as laymen, before and
at the time of the Dissolution.

memorials of later Throckmortons. And so at Ullenhall,[1] near Wootton Wawen, and elsewhere.

Thus the little boy had often been reminded of his heritage, and doubtless he profited much by what he was told and what he saw of all these things. Under such unsettled conditions the matter of his adequate education must have been a difficult one, added to which it would seem that his mother was at that time delicate, and unable to do as much for him as she would have wished. So, at Michaelmas, 1653, Francis then being just thirteen, one James Smyth was appointed to be his steward, thus he is styled. Smyth, who was a well-educated man of mature age and much energy, was to be paid £20 a year, and to be supplied with his diet and lodging, together with money for all necessary expenses. It is to him that we owe these perfectly-kept accounts of, as he himself writes on the first page of his little ledger, "all Receipts and Disbursements for the use of Sir Francis Throckmorton ever since I began to serve him, which was at Michaelmas, 1653"—which accounts are the basis of so much that now follows. Smyth, who in the first months of his service seems almost to have been the fatherless boy's tutor, did indeed—at least for some seven years—become his guide, doubtless his philosopher at times, and always his good friend.

At Coughton Court there was also a folio volume,[2] unfortunately now apparently missing, of "The accounts of the present expenditure of Sir Francis Throckmorton from Michaelmas, 1643, to Lady Day, 1650", his very early years, with which Smyth was definitely not associated.

Francis, who was the only surviving son, for at least two others had died in infancy, now lived with his mother at Weston Underwood—or Weston, as it shall henceforth appear here—near Olney, a delightfully situated Buckinghamshire estate and mansion—Weston House[3]—which had

---

[1] Sir W. Dugdale, *Antiquities of Warwickshire*, (ed. 1765), pp. 576–7, and illustration.

[2] Hist. MSS. Comm., 3rd Report (1872), p. 257.

[3] *Buckinghamshire* (Royal Commission on Historical Monuments), Vol. II, pp. 316–18; Lipscomb, *op. cit.* Vol. IV, p. 403. There was also a priest's hiding-place at Weston House. "This mansion having been erected at various periods, displays no uniformity of style. The principal front was built by Sir Robert Throckmorton, about the beginning of the last century". (James Storer, *The Rural Walks of Cowper* (c. 1840), p. 71).

come into his family through the marriage, in 1446, of Thomas Throckmorton with Margaret, daughter of Robert Olney, who was then seated there. Coughton Court, as already noted, had suffered much during the Civil Wars and was now almost uninhabitable, which was doubtless the reason for this removal to Weston, in which district the Throckmortons also had so many family connexions and congenial friends.

Returning briefly to Sir Robert, he had died at Weston, and just before his death had made his will,[1] on January 13th, 1650-1, appointing his wife as sole executrix, "she to have the use of all my household stuff at Weston House". There is also reference to "household stuff in my two houses at Coughton and Moor Hall", at which latter house Thomas Sheldon was then living. He was the third son of William Sheldon, of Broadway, co. Worcester, and plays quite a prominent part in Smyth's accounts, for it fell to him, on behalf of the estate, to keep Smyth regularly supplied with the necessary funds.

Moor Hall,[2] not far from Coughton, had been in the Throckmorton family for many years, and eventually in 1696 Sir Robert, the third baronet, sold it to Richard Bartlam, of Sheffield, for £1,120. The Bartlams resold the house to the Throckmortons towards the end of the 18th Century, and in 1919 it was purchased by Mr E. A. Cubberley, the father of the present owners, Miss R. Cubberley and Mr Haywood Cubberley.

One of the three overseers of the will was to be "my loving friend, William Sheldon[3] of Beoley, co. Worcester, esquire", head of the influential Worcestershire-Warwickshire family—with which the Throckmortons were connected by marriage—and related to the above Thomas Sheldon. The three witnesses were Lewis Mordaunt, Thomas Terry, steward at Weston, and John Greswold.

[1] P.C.C., 267 Brent. A photostat copy of this will has now been deposited at Birmingham Reference Library.
[2] The late A. C. Coldicott, of Stratford-on-Avon, wrote—in a letter—in August, 1939: "Moor Hall is a most interesting house, the major part now covered with stucco or cement. I have rarely been over a place which provides so many alluring and complex problems on dates and development". See illustration facing p. 79, made from a photograph kindly and specially taken by Mr. F. C. Morgan, F.S.A., in that year.
[3] E. A. B. Barnard, *The Sheldons*, (Chapter V).

Smyth's accounts actually begin at Throckmorton, where Francis had stayed with his mother for brief periods during several years after his father's death. Here, remotely situated, her ladyship at such times kept up some little style at the small ancestral manor-house[1] built by the Throckmortons of the early 14th Century, where nothing would be comparable to the life which had been led at Coughton Court in the good old days.

Thus it was at Throckmorton that Smyth took up his duties, at Michaelmas, 1653, but he does not appear to have been responsible for any expenditure on behalf of Francis—"my master"—until a few months later, the first item being under February 26th, 1653–54. Rather inappropriately for the boy perhaps—but after all the choice of liquid refreshment was then quite limited[2]—it was for a pint of sack[3] and 2 quarts of metheglin,[4] 2s., followed soon after by 3 pints of sack, 1s. 3d., for a glass bottle to carry it, 2d., and for horsemeat,[5] 1s. 4d., when my master was at Worcester, which city was now beginning to make some little recovery after the devastating experiences through which it had so recently passed. To Worcester Francis and Smyth had gone on horseback, jolting uncomfortably along those particularly and notoriously bad roads, for a brief visit, and the latter had no intention of running any risks for either of them with the bad drinking-water which was known to be supplied there, as generally at that period. A little later, when the boy was again upon the road, he and Smyth had beer,[6] which cost 2d. a time.

[1] Near the little church is a moat which probably surrounded the manor-house.

[2] It was not until at least ten years later that tea, coffee, and chocolate could be obtained, and then only in small quantities and seldom outside London.

[3] *Vin sec.* A dry, white wine formerly imported from Spain and the Canary Islands.

[4] Or mead. There are numerous recipes for the making of metheglin or meath as Sir Kenelm calls it, in *The Closet of Sir Kenelm Digby Opened,* (1671), edited by Anne Macdonall, and published in 1910. One of them is "Sir Baynam Throckmorton's Measure". Sir Baynam was the second baronet of the Gloucestershire branch of the family.

[5] Fodder.

[6] At this time synonymous with ale which, apart from its usual purpose, seems to have been taken on any occasion, and for all sorts of ills. Francis had ale for his ague, and Pepys says that he himself drank butter ale for a heavy cold. Animals, too, were copiously drafted with it.

Amongst other items at this time are those for whipcord—for his top—and Jew's trumps,[1] 4d.; Smyth's total expenses, so he says, of 16s. 8d., to Weston, on to London, and home to Throckmorton—altogether a journey, which he took mostly by coach, of some 225 miles; for The History of Guy of Warwick,[2] 6d.; various expenses for mending my master's clothes, 1s. 6d.; and to the barber for trimming my master, 1s. 6d. On returning to Throckmorton there were many things to do, including the purchase of sandiver[3] for the nag's eye, when Smyth rode over to do some shopping at Pershore, near at hand.

Colonel Thomas Throckmorton, an uncle of the boy, now makes his first appearance, the occasion being his association with Smyth in the matter of certain letters of administration with which Smyth served him, and which were concerned with the estate of the late baronet.

A day or two later Francis and Smyth rode over to Coughton Court, not many miles away, where they stayed the night, and then went on to see Warwick Castle,[4] a visit doubtless inspired by the reading of the aforesaid little book. At the Castle a sum of 3s. was distributed among my Lord Brook's[5] servants and the soldiers. Soon they were back again at Throckmorton, where in April, 1654, a wandering piper was given 3d. Then there was music[6] on May Day,

---

[1] Jew's harps, which in some parts of England are still known as Jew's trumps. Samuel Pepys, in his Diary, records that in one of his visits to Vauxhall Gardens, he heard the nightingales, "and", he continues, "here fiddles, there a harp, and here a Jew's trump . . ."

[2] An early edition of The Noble and Renowned History of Guy Earl of Warwick, of which the eighth was published in 1736. "How round the children's eyes would grow as they listened to the gestes of King Arthur and his noble knights, or the doughty deeds of Guy of Warwick!" Elizabeth Godfrey, English Children in the Olden Time, (1907), p. 51.

[3] Glass-gall.

[4] In the following August, John Evelyn, notes in his Diary: "We pass'd next thro' Warwick, and saw the Castle, the dwelling-house of Lord Brook . . . Here they showed us Sir Guy's greate two-handed sword, staff, horse-armes, potts, and other reliques of that famous knight-errant. Warwick is a faire old Towne, and hath one Church full of antient monuments . . ."

[5] This Lord Brook had succeeded, in 1643, to the barony of Brook of Beauchamps Court, Alcester, and Brook of Warwick Castle.

[6] Many payments for music appear in these accounts.

6d.; the May Day mummers were given 2s.; and Mrs. Browne, the lady's maid, was repaid for an ell of holland for socks,[1] 3s. 8d., black thread, 2d., a white drinking-pot, 6d., and cakes, 6d., all purchased on behalf of Francis.

Soon they were off on a short visit to the Salweys—old friends of the Throckmortons—at Stanford, some 13 miles on the other side of Worcester, where the maid for a fairing received 1s., and the other servants had 3s. 9d. to share among them. Spring was now well advanced, and this meant a new suit—its cost is not stated—together with buttons for my master's satin sleeves, 8d., which things were also bought at Pershore. Shortly afterwards they went to Coughton Court, Lady Throckmorton going too, where the bellringers welcomed them, and received 2s., a similar sum being divided among the old almswomen. Mrs Browne also accompanied her ladyship, being a payment made for mending her pillion, and for stuffing 2 saddles before the little party set out.

A few days later they were back, all of them, once more at Throckmorton, where extra washing of linen had to be done for Francis after his dusty travels. Other preparations having been made, he and Smyth again set off for Coughton, and then on to Lord Carington's, another uncle, not far off at Wootton Wawen—past which Charles II had passed in his flight from Worcester, in September 1651— the home of that devoted Warwickshire Royalist who had already suffered so much for his principles.[2] Here they remained for five days, on their departure the servants receiving 15s., and the village poor were not forgotten.

Thence they went to Welford-on-Avon, a few miles away, and so into Northamptonshire, to Rothwell, to Weldon, and then to Deene, all in the Kettering district. At Weldon, where they stayed a day or two, Francis dined with Mrs Saunders, a member of a well-known local family; the ringers rang the church bells; and 8d. was paid for a pint of wine to make Mrs Saunders's maid drink. At Weldon, too, Francis bought cakes, 4d., and a pair of stirrup stockings,[3] 1s. 6d.

[1] See holland stockings, p. 65.
[2] A few years later he was murdered in France by one of his servants, simply for plunder.
[3] See p. 22.

At Deene was the mansion of the Brudenells, and not far distant, at Lyveden, were the Treshams—still very much under the Gunpowder Plot cloud—who, together with the Saunderses, were all more or less related to the Throckmortons. The aforesaid Colonel Thomas Throckmorton, who had served with Charles I, was also at this time living at Deene, where Francis stayed with him for some days, during which time he gave 1s. to the music and to a blind woman, and Lord Brudenell's[1] groom and gardener had each a similar sum, another man receiving 6d. In making his master's gifts Smyth was always careful to consider the degree of those on whom they were bestowed, and distributed them accordingly.

An important conference now took place at Deene as to the boy's immediate future, and the possibilities of Cambridge for his education were explored. The Colonel and Francis were here joined by 'Mr Salwey', a member of the friendly family at Stanford, who often appears thus in the accounts. His Christian name is never given, but actually he was the "Thomas Salwey, of Throckmorton, guardian of Francis Throckmorton, Sir Robert's infant son", who on February 5th, 1651–52, had claimed "discharge of Sir Robert's estate in cos. Warwick, Worcester, and Bucks, descended to Francis, two-thirds whereof are sequestered for recusancy of Sir Robert, who died January 16th, 1651–2".[2] The claim was eventually allowed, and the sequestration discharged.

A day or two later Francis and Salwey went on together to Weston, Smyth of course being with them. Doubtless this journey was taken for the purpose of discussing those important Deene matters with Lady Throckmorton, who almost at once sent off Smyth—who ate the ordinary, for which he paid the usual 6d., at an inn the first day out— to Moor Hall to see Thomas Sheldon about the supply of ready money. He was back again soon afterwards, but meanwhile Francis had taken a step forward in life. His hair was trimmed at Olney, 1s.; he lost at play at Weston,

---

[1] Thomas, Baron Brudenell, who at the Restoration was created Earl of Cardigan.

[2] *Committee for Compounding*, 1643–60. Pt. IV, p. 2710.

B

1s. 6d.—this is the first reference to cards—and he had taken a hand at gleek,[1] losing 2s. Moreover he lost a bet of 2d. at bowls, received 5s. for pocket-money, purchased a hawk,[2] 2s., bought lace for his waistcoat, 2d., received a gift of venison, gave 1s. to the cook at Weston,[3] and called on several friends in the immediate district. Also, during Smyth's absence, he had ridden over to Wellingborough with Salwey, where they drank sack, and remembered the poor. Certain trunks had been left at Weldon, and a servant was now sent to bring them to Weston, there to be ready for the important packing which was soon to take place. August was proceeding apace; Cambridge it was to be; and there was much to be done before the academic year commenced there.

[1] A game of cards, played by three persons with forty-four cards, each hand having twelve, with eight being left for the 'stock'. A gleek was a set of three court cards in the same hand. C. H. Hartman, *Games and Gamesters of the Restoration*, (1930), pp. 44-7.

[2] One of two references to hawking, which appear in these accounts, in which there is no mention of archery, football, or swimming. Fishing is only mentioned once,—and that at Cambridge—although the River Ouse flows just below Weston.

[3] This item, dated June 23rd—Midsummer Eve—suggests that the cook at Weston had a "with" on that day. (See p. 36, *n.* 1; and Brand's *Popular Antiquities*, Vol. I, p. 318).

Chapter II
CAMBRIDGE, SEPTEMBER, 1654—MARCH, 1657-8

The first actual approach to Cambridge comes under August 23rd, 1654, midway through the Commonwealth, during the latter years of which, at least, there is still much to learn concerning the life of the Town and of the University. Cambridge, in comparison with to-day, had then only a small population, a few thousands, living in very cramped quarters.

It is particularly interesting to note that John Evelyn visited Cambridge only a week later when on August 31st, 1654, he has a good deal to say about it all, which he—an Oxford man—concludes thus: "But the whole towne is situate in a low dirty unpleasant place, the streets ill paved, the aire thicke and infected by the Fennes, nor are its churches (of which St Marie's is the best) any thing considerable in compare with those of Oxford".[1]

Some 20 years later, Edward Chamberlayne, in his "Angliae Notitia, or the Present State of England" (Pt. II, p. 323), says: "What hath been said of Oxford, the like may be said of her sister, Cambridge, which for antiquities, gracious Priviledges, beautiful Colleges, large Revenues, good Discipline, number of students, plenty of Diet, and of all other things necessary for advancement of learning (if in complaisance she will at any time give place to Oxford yet at the same time) will challenge precedence before any other University of the Christian World".

Francis was now nearly fourteen. As a Roman Catholic, and the heir of a recusant, he could not of course gain admission to the University, but must be content to abide on its fringes, and live the academic life as far as was possible under such conditions.[2] Preparations must now be made

---

[1] Inversely, the more magnanimous Pepys, when he visited Oxford in 1668, thought it "a mighty fine place". He had taken his degree from Magdalene College, Cambridge, in 1653.

[2] In any case his title, at least as such, would have been denied recognition, for in November, 1643, Parliament had declared void all honours conferred by Charles I since May 22, 1642, on those in opposition to it. A little later this period was further reduced.

on the spot, and so to Cambridge Smyth went to make all
the preliminary arrangements for his young master's arrival
there.　He duly noted all his own relevant expenses, which
were not many, and included the shoeing, 4d., of his horse
on the road thither.　His expenses in the town for one day
and night amounted to 3s., with an additional 1s. 10d. for
horsemeat.　This was at the old Rose Inn,[1] where Francis
himself stayed on several later occasions.　Smyth also
entertained one Mr Bagley who assisted him in his business,
on whom he spent 3s., Bagley appears again soon afterwards
as tutor to Francis.[2]

Later in the summer Smyth paid a second visit to Cambridge, his expenses this time being 7s. 6d. for one night and
two days.　Then came much preparation at Weston,
including the purchase for Francis—at Olney—of two pairs
of shoes, 6s., and lace for his night-caps, 2s., the mending of
some of his clothes costing 6d.　There was also music on
his birthday (September 13th), followed by the repayment
of 2s. to a certain Monsieur Kiro, a horse-doctor, which sum
he was paid for curing my master's nag; expenses, 1s., on a
journey to Eaton[3] with Mr Mordaunt[4] undertaken by
Smyth; and 1s. for ale at Yardley Old or Oak, the ladies
being there.　This was the famous Yardley Oak,[5] always a
favourite rendezvous of visitors to Yardley Forest, a few
miles from Weston.

On September 29th Smyth paid yet a third visit to Cambridge, this time bringing with him both Salwey and Thomas

---

[1] Familiar to Pepys, who slept badly there one night a few years
later, "by reason of some drunken scholars making a noise all night".
[2] See p. 22.
[3] Eaton Socon, close to the Bedfordshire-Huntingdonshire border.
[4] Lewis Mordaunt (see p. 1, _n._ 1), who was connected with the Mordaunts of Turvey, nor far from Weston.　He was going to Eaton
Socon, to reach Bushmead Priory, a short distance away, where his
relatives the Gerys, lived.　See V. C. H. _Bedfordshire_, Vol. III,
pp. 147–8.
[5] V. C. H. _Northants_, Vol. II, 351, and frontispiece, Vol. IV;
Storer, _op. cit._, pp. 40–1.　In later days Yardley Oak was particularly
associated with William Cowper, the poet, who was a great friend
of the Throckmortons of his Weston period.　One of the rooms in
the Cowper Museum at Olney is named after them, and contains
relics associated with them.　The original manuscript of some of
the poet's hymns and letters is still preserved at Coughton Court.

Sheldon. Under the will of Sir Robert Throckmorton, they were the appointed guardians of the boy, and had of course come to Cambridge to approve the arrangements that Smyth had made. The little party arrived at the time of the famous Stourbridge Fair[1]—it may have provided John Bunyan with the idea of his Vanity Fair[2]—to which they of course went, and Smyth, on behalf of the absent Francis, paid 3s. for 6 napkin-hooks given by my master for fairings—a favourite gift with him—and also 8d. for a pair of gloves. Their stay was naturally very brief, and having satisfied themselves with the Cambridge arrangements they all returned to Weston, their total expenses having amounted to £3 11s. 1d. Shortly afterwards preparations were seriously made for Francis himself to begin his great adventure. The day before they started Smyth advanced him 1s. 6d. for pocket-money on the road, his clothes were again mended, and a pair of winter shoes for him cost 3s.

At last the great day—October 9th—dawned, and a necessarily early start was made in the old family coach-and-four, with the trunks packed tightly away in the fore and hind boots. It was 45 miles to Cambridge, and Turvey, only a few miles distant from Weston, made a pleasant stopping-place—one of several on the way—for here lived the Mordaunts,[3] or at least Mrs Henry Mordaunt, who entertained the party, her servants receiving 6s. from Francis, who was always thoughtful in these matters. In addition to Smyth, Francis was accompanied by his ubiquitous boy, Jack Parsons, who remained for a long time in his service, and there was the coachman too, who drove the empty coach back to Weston the next day.

[1] The Fair began on the feast of St Bartholomew (Aug. 24th) and continued till the 14th day after the feast of the Exaltation of the Holy Cross (Sept. 14th). It was here that a few years later in 1661, Isaac Newton—then a freshman at Trinity College—bought his famous prism. That same year, on Sept. 19th, Pepys and his wife "rode through Sturbridge fayre, but the fayre was almost over".

[2] He was then just becoming known as a preacher in the Bedford-Olney district.

[3] The Mordaunts, who are represented by some fine tombs in Turvey church, had entered into English history on a number of occasions, and Henry Mordaunt had been sent to the Tower under suspicion of being concerned in the Gunpowder Plot, but was fined and released.

On arrival at Cambridge that evening Francis, with
Smyth and Parsons, went straight to the lodgings (Lee's)—
with diet, or board—which Smyth had already taken for
them, the coachman putting up at an unnamed inn, where his
expenses for the night came to 3s. The horsemeat there
for that night cost as much as 6s. 8d., probably including the
stabling charges, which are not mentioned.

But what an affair "coming up" and "going down", with
all their attendant difficulties and complexities, must have
been then, and of course much more so in earlier times!
Well, here they were at last, and the first thing Francis
then did on the following morning was to send off greetings
to his mother in the form of oysters,[1] 2s. 4d., to Weston;
and his next thought—or more probably it was Smyth's—
was for sugar and for candles,[2] 1 lb. for 5d., to help lighten
those dismal and darksome conditions of which the lengthen-
ing autumn evenings were already a forcible reminder.
The Cambridge autumn-winter scene of those days can only
be imagined.

This was the first time that young Francis had ever come
to Cambridge and, always of an enquiring mind, he was
eager to go sight-seeing that day, King's College Chapel
being first in his thoughts, where he gave the clerk 1s., and
the College butler received 6d. for some unstated reason.
Later in the day he played billiards[3]—then very popular and,
of course, very different to our modern billiards—but there
is no record as to where he played his game, or games,
which cost him 10d. The following day there was a visit
to John Angier's, the tailor—Pepys's "my cozen Angier"

[1] Colchester oysters had been coming to Cambridge since at least
the year 1380. There is plenty of 17th–19th century evidence of
the sending of oysters as presents to relations and friends, and of how
often they deteriorated in transit, sometimes the whole barrel being
bad on arrival.

[2] Candles are often mentioned, but there is never any mention of
a tinder-box or snuffers.

[3] A few years later, Charles Cotton, in his *The Compleat Gamester*,
(1674), says: "The gentele, cleanly, and most ingenious game of
Billiards . . . is much approved of and plaid by most nations in
Europe, especially in England, there being few towns of note therein
which hath not a publick billiard table, neither are they wanting in
many noble and private families in the country for the recreation of
the mind and the exercise of the body".

The Tower of London, Commanded in Chief by the R. Hon.ble Robert L'Lucas

THE TOWER OF LONDON, c. 1695

(From the Pepsian Collection, Magdalene College, Cambridge)

was very well-known to the Cambridge of his day—for a suit and cloak, £9 1s. 9d., as appears by the bills of particulars, which Smyth does not detail. There are, however, full particulars of another suit made at Cambridge a little later on.

Francis, in addition to constant colds and intermittent attacks of ague—which naturally seem to have been more frequent under the climatic conditions of Cambridge—also suffered from weak eyes, as is evidenced by various and recurring items of expenditure, amongst them now being one for sack and for ale to wash my master's eyes, repeated a few days later. His eyes, however, were never in such a condition that he had to be bled for them, as was Pepys not long afterwards. Indeed there is no mention of actual bleeding throughout these accounts, except of horses. That same day he purchased a lecture book, 6d., some writing-paper, an inkhorn, a pencil, ink, and a paper-book, 2s. 1d. altogether.

No time was lost in paying a visit to the Printing House— of which in these present days the University Press is the great outcome—where he gave 1s. as a gift for being shown round—and afterwards went, thus Smyth records, to Hogmagog Hills,[1] at that time a particularly favourite riding expedition with undergraduates, which cost him only 8d. for refreshments. The hire of the horse was 6d.,[2] about which there was surely nothing to complain, except perhaps as to the horse.

Letters were now despatched to relatives and friends, and within a fortnight of his arrival Francis entertained Mr Smith[3] of King's and the dancing-master to dinner, in connection with which the only detailed expenses are of 10d.

[1] This had become a fairly common 17th Century form—of brief duration—of spelling Gogmagog Hills, but would seem to have disappeared before the close of that era. The road from Cambridge to the Gogmagogs was at that time particularly bad, and so remained until c. 1723 in which year a subscription list was sent round, to raise funds for its repair, which proved successful. The original list (Doc. 1670) is preserved at Cambridge University Library.
[2] The cost of horse-hiring was, as a general rule, relatively very small at this period.
[3] There was a contemporary John Smith, a Fellow of King's, who had Warwickshire associations.

for a quart of claret, and 1s. for a quart of white wine. At the same time Smyth handed him 3s. as ready-money for the card-playing which followed. He had not been at Cambridge long when in mid-November he caught a cold and spent 1s. 1d. on pectoral lozenges, or trochies[1], as Smyth usually styles them. Candles and yet more candles were needed, and the purchase of playing-cards, whip-top,[2] glue, and more writing-paper helped to make up the expenses for that week. Shortly afterwards another whip-top, this time together with the scourge for it, cost 2d.

The following week Francis had evidently recovered, and had decided to go to London. So a Cambridge coach, £1 10s., was hired, for which the customary earnest of 10s. was deposited; and marmalade—made of quinces—macaroons, 1s. 6d., and wine, 1s 6d., were bought to take in the coach when my master went towards London[3] but, as will shortly appear, had soon to return from whence he came. Gratuities were given to the coachman and to the ostler, whilst the poor—the then usual accompaniment at such a setting-forth—were represented by a few clamorous souls dodging around the coach, ostensibly to wish the travellers a good journey as they prepared to depart, to whom Francis gave 6d. amongst them. This adventure, late in November, for some unstated reason proved unfortunate, for the travellers got no farther than Sawston Inn— probably the King's Head—some 7 miles from Cambridge, where certain expenses were incurred on behalf of Smyth and Parsons, whilst my master lodged one night at the Hall. Here he may have had a cordial welcome from the old squire, Henry Huddleston, the head of the only Roman Catholic family then in the district. He was, however, at that time 78 years old, and therefore the entertaining was

[1] Flat round tablets.

[2] It would seem possible that Francis purchased whip-tops, as he did on more than one occasion, in order to provide himself with some form of indoor exercise in bad weather. This was undoubtedly done by young people in the long galleries of some 17th Century country houses, e.g. Chastleton, co. Oxford.

[3] As far on as 1792, at which time a journey of a hundred miles was considered as an undertaking of time, privation, and endurance, the coach from Cambridge to London—55 miles—took nine hours to reach its destination, under normal conditions.

more probably done by his son, also named Henry.[1] During that evening at the Hall Francis played cards, losing 3s. 6d.

The next day gratuities amounting to 4s. 6d. were given to Mr Huddleston's servants, and other Sawston expenses included a quart of claret, 1s., at the inn, and a similar payment for horsemeat, an item which in those days appears never to have been included in the cost of hiring a coach. The party then returned to Cambridge, but Francis was not to be denied, and a week or so later they all set out again by hired coach for London, the poor again being with them at the moment of their departure. This time a servant accompanied them on a nag. They stopped the night at an inn at Bishop's Stafford—thus Smyth writes Bishops Stortford[2]—where the expenses amounted to 11s. 8d., exclusive of 1s. 6d. for the coachman. It is to be hoped that their inn was not the Reindeer, much frequented by Cambridge travellers, and kept about that time by the notorious Elizabeth Aynsworth—formerly well-known to the University authorities—whom Pepys also mentions.

Francis stayed at his mother's lodgings—the detailed expenses are given—in London for a few days. There, if these accounts be any guide, he does not appear to have had a very exciting time on this occasion, his chief distractions being a visit to the Old Exchange—then a good shopping-centre[3]—and to the Tower. This visit to the Tower— perhaps made with his ill-fated namesake in mind—was rather expensive, for the hackney coach[4] cost 6s.; given at the Tower, 6s.; expenses there, 1s. 6d.; and the chain-keeper—one has visions of Francis and the lions, or it may have been at the drawbridge—received one penny, only that.

During this visit he drank a little ale instead of wine on fasting nights, and also in the mornings.

Then, on December 13th, came the return to Cambridge, costing £1 for coach-hire, with 2s. to the coachman for both

---

[1] He succeeded to the encumbered estates in 1657. T. F. Teversham, *History of Sawston*, Part I, p. 39.

[2] As also did Pepys.

[3] In day-time the shops were very much open, glass windows and doors not being supplied to them until some years afterwards.

[4] A four-wheeled coach for hire, usually drawn by a pair of horses, and seated for six persons.

stages, the first one being Bishop's Stortford as before, where the night's expenses came to 11s. 5d., dinner at Newport (Essex), halfway on the second stage the next day, costing 3s.   Directly Francis was back at Cambridge another cold came on, and several supplies of lozenges and syrups were obtained.   Some more nightcaps were also made for his better protection from the bad draughts in Mr Lee's tumble-down old house—with its thin walls—in which he was lodging.

The cold being cured Francis, now more cheerful, bought two pennyworth of ballads,[1] and Smyth paid £1 5s. to the dancing-master for my master's entrance.   Christmas Day came, but with it no reference to the festival[2]—indeed there is scarcely any reference to a Church festival throughout the accounts—but 6d. given to the music that day may denote a mild observance somewhere in the town.

Two days afterwards Francis dined with Mr Wiborow, probably Thomas Wiborow[3] of Queens' and St Catharine's, Vicar of Impington—a Pepys stronghold—near Cambridge, from 1639 to c. 1656 and again from 1662 to 1669.   He had a private school in the town, and was instructing Francis in some unstated subject.

On January 1st,[4] 1654–55, a New Year's gift was brought from Weston to Francis, for which service the bearer was given 2s.   Shortly afterwards Francis went to stay for five days in Bedfordshire with another of the Mordaunts, who was living at Everton, near Sandy, horses being hired, 8s., to take him and Parsons there and back.   Returning to

---

[1] Pepys's unique collection of contemporary broadside ballads (approximately 1800 of them) in five folio volumes, is in the Pepysian Library, Magdalene College.

[2] There was, of course, no Roman Catholic church at Cambridge after the Reformation until some 80 years ago, and then only a small one.   The present church of Our Lady and the English Martyrs was consecrated on October 8th, 1890, on which occasion some serious misgivings arose in certain circles by the fact that the bells of Great St Mary's—the University Church—pealed joyfully during that afternoon.   Feelings were allayed, however, when enquiry revealed that the bells had been actually rung to signalize, as was then customary, the appointment of a new Professor.

[3] Dr J. A. Venn, *Alumni Cantabrigienses*, Pt. I, Vol. IV, p. 481.

[4] January 1st, already popularly regarded as New Year's Day, and not the then official March 25th.

Cambridge, he again dined with his tailor—the aforesaid Angier—and gave the waiting-maid 1s. In January, amongst other things purchased were Aesop's Fables, a paper-book, and a phrase-book,[1] whilst 1s. was paid for bringing Helm's Geography,[2] thus styled, from Weston.

On January 18th a gift of 6s. was made to the Town Music,[3] or Waits, that played by night in the winter—in the streets, and by torchlight and lanthornlight—and a week later 2s. 6d. to the music belonging to the dancing-school. Shortly afterwards 6d. was given to more music; 1s. to the University Music; the Town Music was again rewarded on several occasions during that winter; and 2s. 6d. went to music unspecified on Shrove Tuesday.

During February there was much attention to the personal appearance and appointments of my master. He went to the barber—18d. a time—twice in five weeks; had his watch mended, 8d.; and bought—amongst other things—a pair of shoes, 3s. 6d.; a box and peas,[4] 3d., ribbons[5] for his suit, curling-irons for his wig—which he seems to have seldom worn, although he was careful to keep his hair closely trimmed—4d., another pair of shoes, 3s. 4d.; and some stirrup-leathers, to hang the stirrups from the saddle. In this month he also played billiards and cards; lost at ball[6]; paid for sack and claret; and bought a double sheath for his knives, probably a pair of knives which he used at table. The dancing-master was paid the usual £1 5s. for a quarter's instruction at the dancing-school, and 2s. 6d. was given to the music there. Then there was as much as 10s. 8d. for an ell (45 inches) of holland to make my master's bands—his

---

[1] A book in which phrases or the idioms of a language—probably French in this case—are collected and explained.

[2] This work is not to be found in the Royal Geographical Society's Library, or elsewhere.

[3] On the occasion of one of his visits to Cambridge, a few years later, Pepys was met by the Town Music, "but Lord! what sad music they made!" he adds. *v.* also references in C. H. Cooper's *Annals of Cambridge*, Vols. III and IV.

[4] Perhaps a puzzle.

[5] The elaborate use of ribbons was just then very fashionable, *e.g.* p. 43.

[6] Tennis.

many collars, or ruffs, and his cuffs, which were kept in a bandbox—and 6s. for the making of them. The month was approaching its close when for a duck to hunt on the river —presumably a decoy duck trained to lure others into a trap—1s. was given.

On March 13th, 1654–55, Francis went to the Cambridge Quarter Sessions—this is the first hint that he was actually studying Law, and thus was now interested in Court procedure—and he also purchased a paper-book and writing-paper, 1s., a Calapeia,[1] 1s. 6d., paste-board, more paper, and the oft-recurring pair—and sometimes pairs—of gloves which he presented to relatives and friends.

Then there must be a new suit, so Angier again made one for him, as also a cloak, which together cost £8 7s. 6d. This expense, however, did not include the buttons, for 16s. had to be paid for 8 dozen buttons for his suit; 1s. 6d. for a neck-button and loop-lace; and 1s. for a waist-button. The making of the suit and cloak cost 13s. 9d., the tailor's man receiving his customary 6d. when they were duly delivered.

On March 28th, 1655, 1s. was given to a man that had strange beasts to show, this item being preceded and followed by various small payments for claret. On April 10th Lee's —his landlord—bill for diet etc. was paid. Its items, which amounted to £42 1s. 9d., included wood for the fires, £3 9s. 9d.; half a year's diet for my master and for his servants, £36; entertainment[2] of friends invited by Francis at several times, 15s.; 17 meals for strangers, 17s.; and washing of his linen for half-a-year, £1. In addition, 6s. 6d. was given to Lee's servants.[3]

---

[1] *Calepin.* A polyglot dictionary. From Ambrosio Calepino, of Calepio, in Italy, the author of a famous Latin Dictionary, first published in 1502. There are many editions of it in the Cambridge University Library. Evelyn, under the year 1662—in his *Chalcography*, eventually published in 1769—says: "We have weeded the calepines and lexicons". (*N.E.D.*).

[6] There is never any reference to visits to either of the Cambridge coffee-houses, the Greek's Head and the Turk's Head, then becoming popular places of resort.

[3] There were also payments to tubmen—they are not thus styled in these accounts—for the sanitary service which they, and sometimes women too, undertook in those days.

A few days later Francis again went to the Mordaunts at Everton, and then home to Weston. Thence he went to Olney Fair where he spent 4s., and again bought some ballads, 2d.; and also to Tyringham, a parish without a village, not far from Weston and about 3 miles from Newport Pagnell. The visit to Tyringham House—the home for centuries of the Tyringhams—was made in order to attend a cock-fight; on that same day Smyth gave 2s. to the ringers of the church bells[1] of Weston; and 4d. to the clerk when my master did ring, which he did whenever he got the least chance.

However all this was not Cambridge, to which Francis soon returned by way of Bedford and St Neots, his baggage being brought on a sumpter-horse. At St Neots the expenses for the night were 19s., and there he visited the church, and the poor had their usual dole. His Cambridge life now makes a somewhat tardy reappearance. On April 25th a writing-desk, of which he later lost the key, was purchased, 3s. 4d., followed by an Ovid de Tristibus, 9d., Petrarch's Works, 2s. 4d., a music-book, 2s. 6d., and exercise paper, 6d. Sometimes he also supplied himself with book-strings, or book-ribbons for use in his books. Then there were more visits to colleges, the butler of Trinity receiving 6d., Clare Hall servants 9d., and the clerk of King's Chapel 6d.

A little later there were payments for currant-wormseed and a gallipot for it, 8d., bird-seed, 4d., and a bird-cage, 1s. 6d., and ultimately—on July 5th—there was brought to Lee's house, a bird that did sing several tunes, 15s., and a nest of linnets, 3d. A few weeks afterwards a pennyworth of seeds, for the bird only, suggests that the linnets had not long survived. After that there is a significant silence concerning these bird-affairs.

Then, as to other Cambridge entertainment, about this time Francis played and lost 1s. 10d. at bowls,[2] bought a bowl and nine-pins, lost 1s. at shovel-board,[3] went on July

---

[1] Replaced by a new set in 1687.
[2] "The insipid pastime of bowls", as John North, afterwards Master of Trinity, wrote soon after the Restoration.
[3] Then being rapidly displaced in popularity by billiards.

5th to see a stage-play, 3s., and gave 1s. to Mr Tyringham's man that brought him a cock, so evidently the visit to the cock-fight at Tyringham was to have its repercussions at Cambridge. Above all, despite the general order for its suppression made just then, he had been to a bear-baiting[1]— but probably not on Market Hill, where for so many years this degrading pastime had been associated with Shrove Tuesday—and to the Physick or Physical Garden,[2] on May 9th. About this time he also bought a horse-lock, 10d., a pair of Spanish leather shoes, 3s., and a pair of stirrup stockings[3] to set to silk tops, 1s.

On July 7th Francis gave £2 to Mr Bagley,[4] his tutor, and on the same day there is a piquant item of 1s. 3d. which this genial and daring youth paid for wine and biscuits to entertain the Proctor.[5] It has already been apparent that he had been away from Cambridge a good deal during the late spring and early summer, and Smyth now records the payment of £7 16s. 6d. to Lee, in full for our diet, my master being in the country a great part of this quarter. Lee was also paid 9s. for a dinner for 3 gentlemen; 15s. for increase for our diet; £2 for hire of our [Cambridge] chambers—the

[1] There is an interesting account of a bear-baiting at Chesterton, in April, 1581, which ended by one of the bedels being "violently thrust and shoved upon the Beare, in such sort that he could hardly keepe himself from hurt". (Arthur Gray, *The Town of Cambridge*, (1925), pp. 104–5).

[2] "A proposal to lay out a Botanic Garden had been made in 1588 by John Gerard, author of the celebrated *Herbal*, to William Cecil, Lord Burleigh, then Chancellor of the University, but it is doubtful if the suggestion was ever conveyed to the University . . ." (Willis and Clark, *Arch. Hist. of Univ. of Cambridge*, Vol. III, p. 146 n. 3). Smyth's reference would seem to show otherwise, and that there was a Physic Garden at Cambridge at least a century previous to Dr Walker's donation of a Botanic Garden to the University in 1764. The Garden to which Francis went in 1655 must have disappeared not long afterwards, for in 1695–6, John Eachard, Master of St Catharine's Hall, was busy with a new scheme for one.

[3] High stockings turned over above the knee.

[4] "Mr [William] Bagley, Minister or curate of Barnewell and St Peters, and one of the Conducts of Kings Colledge", died on March 2nd, 1665. (*Ald. Newton's Diary*, p. 12). He came of a Warwickshire family, and had also been Chaplain of King's. (Venn, *op. cit.*, Pt. I, Vol. I, p. 67).

[5] The Proctors during that academic year were William Fayerbrother, Fellow of King's, and Charles Mildmay, Fellow of Peterhouse. Probably Fayerbrother, the Senior Proctor—a Royalist who had been taken prisoner at Naseby in 1645—was this guest.

only time the rooms were thus styled—in my master's absence, they being reserved for him; and 13s. for Mr Sheldon's diet and those servants that came for my master and brought him back, and for Sir William Andros,[1] one meal. These payments, concerning which there seems to have been a little trouble, being discharged, Francis and those with him removed from Lee's to Lilley's house—1s. being paid for porterage of the trunks.

Later in July he drove over, for the day, to see his friends the Nevilles, at Audley End House,[2] near Saffron Walden, taking with him Lilley[3] and his wife, and Simons,[4] the dancing master, and afterwards they all visited Saffron Walden church, where the sexton was given 6d.

About this time Wyeth, the barber, was paid a part of £4, which fee was due to him for teaching of Jack Parsons to trim his young master who, a little later on, was supplied with 1 lb. of hair-powder, 1s., together with a box for it, 1s. 6d. Amongst other things two pennyworth of diapalma[5] was purchased. On September 1st Francis lost 1s. 6d. at tennis—its first definite mention—and that same day he spent a similar sum on boat-hire to Chesterton, then a small down-river village, little dreaming of that far-off day when it would be incorporated with Cambridge.

On September 9th he went on horseback to Stourbridge Fair—a mile or so away—his first visit, whither he was accompanied by Bagley and Simons. At the Fair 1s. 10d. was given to the poor and puppet-plays and tumblers.[6]

[1] Of Denton, co. Northampton. He held property at Weston, (*Committee for Compounding*, Vol. III, pp. 1739–41).

[2] Evelyn, when he visited Audley End in 1664, described it as being "one of the stateliest palaces in the kingdom". Two years later it attracted Charles II who, as Pepys records, was then contemplating its purchase, a transaction which did not go well.

[3] See footnote on page 35.

[4] Pepys, under June 9th, 1661, refers to a "Mr Symons, (dancing-master) that goes to sea with my Lord [Sandwich]", quite possibly this Cambridge Simons.

[5] A desiccating or detersive plaster, composed originally of palm oil, litharge, and sulphate of zinc. (*O.E.D.*).

[6] Daniel Defoe, in the course of his long account of Stourbridge Fair, which he visited *c.* 1723, says: "Towards the latter end of the Fair . . . the Gentry come in from all parts of the Country round; and though they come for their Diversion; yet 'tis not a little money they lay out, which generally falls to the Retailers, such as Toy-shops, Goldsmiths, Brasiers, Ironmongers, Milleners, Mercers, etc., and some loose Coins, they reserve for the Puppet Shows, Drolls, Rope-Dancers, and such like . . ."

There he also spent 3s. on his friends, one of whom must have remained but a short time, for later in the day Smyth paid for only 2 dinners in the fair, costing the comparatively large sum of 10s. 8d.   Bagley's man that walked the horses, whilst waiting for his gentlemen, was given 4d., and 4s. 6d. was spent on Lilley's daughters and servants for fairings. That same day there was a payment of 6s. for band-strings.[1]

On September 13th, being his birthday—he was now fifteen—there was some entertainment of friends, 12s., and wine, 6s., for the occasion; and a standish—which had its inkpot and sandbox—cost 2s. 4d.

The next day there was more tennis—again lost—followed by the drinking of sack[2] at a Mrs Walgrove's.   Other items about this time included ingredients for a red plaster,[3] 4s. 7d.; given at a show, 1s. ; a looking-glass and comb-case, 1s.; and some shuttle-cocks, 3d., but no battledore.

Life at Cambridge for the rest of the month seems naturally to have been quiet, the great Fair being over.   However, in October Francis was again paying to the Town Music, and being taught music at £8 a year, arranging for dancing-lessons, seeing the sword-fish, 3d., and buying strings for his viol, 2s. 6d., which he was then being taught in addition to the violin, for which some strings cost 2s.   There follows the expense of 14s. for a wheel for my lady—his mother—living quietly at Weston, and quite probably now and then smoking[4] her pipe as she spun—to whom he gave this spinning-wheel.

The evenings were now getting in, and so there was considerable purchasing of billets of wood for the fires.   About

---

[1] Strings going across the breast for tying in an ornamental way.

[2] Lady Paston writing to her son, William, at Corpus Christi College, Cambridge, in June, 1624, says "Beware of violent tennising; Drink no wine this year, or a very little" she says; and in 1626: "Some do use to heat themselves very much with it [tennis] and then drink burnt sack or such like".   The Master of Corpus (Dr Samuel Walsall), who was accustomed to read all young Paston's letters, afterwards wrote to Lady Paston: "I perceive your ladyship feared his excess at tennis, though I am persuaded there is not any exercise more wholesome, and not many more gentlemanlike".   ("Correspondence of Lady Katherine Paston, 1603–1627", edited with Introduction and Notes by Ruth Hughey.   Norfolk Record Soc., Vol. XIV, pp. 71 and 87).

[3] Red lead in oil on leather, perhaps for an ulcer.

[4] See p. 51.

this time Francis had a coat made, for which seven dozen buttons, 10s. 6d., were supplied. This may have been in due preparation for November 1st, when 4d. was paid for fire at the drawer's when my master's picture was drawn. Unfortunately the name of the drawer, who was probably also engaged on other Cambridge portraits at that time, is not given. A little later on there was beer at the picture-drawer's, 4d., and he was paid £5 1s. for his work.[1] Finally, on December 3rd, a case[2] for the picture cost 8s. Apparently, however, the picture was not completed until the end of the year, when a servant from Weston was sent to fetch it, whose expenses going for my master's picture to Cambridge came to 5s.

About this time Francis also ordered a striking waistcoat of scarlet serge, lined with tabby[3] and silk, and adorned with silver lace, many buttons, and galloon[4] for the binding, the whole costing £1 10s. 2d. Other things then purchased for his personal use included 1¼ yards of cloth for a close coat,[5] and for silk to make it, boots, shoes, and slippers, eight bands and four caps, 2 pairs of Jersey stockings,[6] riding boothose tops,[7] two pairs of shoestrings, some quill pens, a washing-ball, and the usual lozenges. A little later 6d. was given at a bull-baiting, and 3d. to an itinerant bagpiper.

On January 1st, 1655-6, the customary New Year's gifts in money were distributed—amongst the recipients being five children—at Weston, whither Francis, with Smyth and Parsons, had gone just before Christmas, and where he at once had medical attention from Dr Medford, of Olney, whose fee was £1. During the vacation letters came from Cambridge on several occasions, for bringing which the carrier of Olney received 1s. 6d. Various games of cards

[1] In June, 1662, Pepys in London paid "Savill the painter . . for my little portrait", £3.
[2] Frame.
[3] Coarse silk taffety, watered or waved.
[4] A kind of ribbon or tape of silk.
[5] A close-bodied coat.
[6] Of Jersey worsted, which was sometimes also bought for mending his stockings.
[7] The turned-down top part of boothose. "His lacquey with a linen stock on one leg, and a kersey boot-hose on the other . . ." Shakespeare, *Taming of the Shrew*, III, ii, 68.

were played, and there was more church bell-ringing at the village church. Then the three returned to Cambridge, the horses being sent back to Weston the next day. The weather was very cold, and a woman where my master warmed himself on the way received 6d.

The day after his return to Cambridge, 3s. was paid for tobacco which Francis gave away. He himself does not appear at any time to have been a smoker, although smoking had now become very popular[1] with both sexes. He certainly was not prejudiced however, and on at least one later occasion presented tobacco, 1s., to his mother, and at times made similar gifts to other people. Other payments in these early days of the new term included a cat-staff,[2] a Quintus[3] in Latin and one in English—the latter doubtless being a useful addition—4s., a small loss at cards, and given to the University Music, 10s.

Dancing, still under the instruction of Simons, continues to be prominent in the expenses throughout the term, but Francis must have been temporarily incapacitated in March, for a certain Mr Day was paid 1s. for cutting the nail of my master's toe that grew into the flesh. Oranges, probably from Spain, now make their first appearance. Amongst other items at this time—and there were many in connexion with new clothes, and with mending, scouring and altering his old clothes, out of which he was now growing—appear marmalade and sugar cakes, 1s., another top—this time it is called a casting-top—3d., comfits and marcaroons, 1s., and various small losses at tennis and cards, 4s. 4d.

Early in April, Francis paid another visit to Audley End, where this time he stayed with the Nevilles for three days. On leaving he gave the servants 11s., and 6s. was paid for

---

[1] If Barnaby Rich may be credited—in his *Honestie of the Age*—there were, as early as 1614, seven thousand shops in London where tobacco was sold. Smoking already seems to have been fairly general at Cambridge, and of course when James I came in March, 1614–15, it had been officially ordered that "no Graduate, Scholler, or Student of this Universitie . . . doe presume to take tobacco in St Maries Church or Trinity College Hall". See also *Tobacco: Its History and Associations*, F. W. Fairholt, (1876).

[2] A cat-stick for the game of tip-cat.

[3] Probably the *De rebus gestis Alexandri Magni* of Curtius Rufus (Quintus).

		li.	s.	d
For a Mapstik hoork		00.	00.	06.
To mr Hudlestons man		00.	00.	06.
for paper		00.	00.	04
28. For a bird cage		00.	01.	06
Lost att Bowlles		00.	01.	10.
For a pr of shooes		00.	03.	04
Junij. 1. For a pr of gloues		00.	01.	06
To Iegg Barbe		00.	01.	06
For a Bowle & Nine pins		00.	02.	06
For stirrop lethers to sett to silke toppes		00.	01.	00.
To mr Lees seruants		00.	04.	00.
To the Clarke of kings Chappell		00.	00.	06.
4. My mrs Housemeate		00.	06.	00.
For 4 horses meate att Cambridge one night		00.	05.	04
Exp: from Cambridge to Bueston		00.	00.	10.
To mr Jerringhams man that braught a Coste		00.	01.	00.
Lost att Shuffle boord by my mr		00.	01.	00.
To my Lord of Northamptons Coreman		00.	05.	00.
To the boy that braught his Nag from Ashby		00.	00.	06
To the Clerke of Weston Churre		00.	00.	06
To Musick p reward of a pesant 6d		00.	01.	06.
To the men that digged the well in the wathouse		00.	00.	06
18. For a pr of bootes and a pr of shoots		00.	13.	00.
July 3. To Iames Sturdy		00.	02.	00.
To Iart Baker		00.	00.	06
For Beer for my mr goeing to Cambridge		00.	00.	03
Exp att St Neots then & in Cambridge att my mrs first comeinge		00.	06.	11.
Ion Ierries exp comming wth the Sumpter & his and Ion Crane Exp. one night in Cambr		00.	04.	04.
To the Barbor		00.	01.	06
5. For horsmeat in Cambridge		00.	12.	06
For Bird that did sing seuerall tunes		00.	15.	00
For a neast of Linott		00.	00.	03
Giuen to see a stage play		00.	03.	00

The totall of this page — 05. 00. 05.

PAGE FROM SMYTH'S LEDGER, MAY–JULY, 1655

horsemeat and for shoeing, before my master came back to Cambridge. Shortly after his return he took a friend, John Smith,[1] to see the colleges, 1s. 6d., and that same day again gave as an earnest for coach-hire, 10s., another visit to London being contemplated. Thither he went on April 12th, Lilley's man that kept my master's seat in the coach, to make sure of it, receiving 6d., and the servants 2s. 6d., on his departure. The first stage was to Bishop's Stortford where, as before, Francis and Smyth stayed for the night, which cost 11s. 10d. They arrived in London the next day.

At this juncture the accounts temporarily become much more detailed, for in London they had to supply their own diet, which it is apparent that they did quite abundantly. Lodgings were taken for them by one Johnson, who seems to have been somewhat of a courier. He had gone up from Cambridge in advance, and met them at the appointed inn when the coach reached London. Thence he took them in a hackney-coach to their lodgings, where they had supper, which consisted of pigeons, followed by roast beef, which together with bread—there is no reference to any vegetables —cheese-cakes, tarts, and oranges, was accompanied by the consumption of some cock ale.[2] Good things were also to follow during the succeeding days, including many salads and radishes, and Francis saw the dancing-horses—who knows where?—played at cards, went out riding in the parks with several of his friends, and also visited the Still-yard,[3] Covent Garden, Shoe Lane—where there was a cock-fighting pit—the Old Bailey, and the Temple. Francis now made his first appearance at the Mulberry Garden—to which fuller reference is made later on—and here he some-what royally entertained an un-named lady. He also took one of the Guldeford ladies—to which family further reference

[1] Apparently a relative of John Smith of King's College, (p. 15).

[2] Cock ale. "Ale mixed with the jelly or minced meat of a boiled cock, besides other ingredients". (*O.E.D.*). During the course of these accounts there are also sundry references to bottle-ales, butter-ale, and small-ale, all being more or less familiar terms; but china-ale, Francis-ale, and goat-ale, which are also mentioned, still require adequate explanation.

[3] The Stillyard or Steelyard, in Upper Thames Street, at that time the meeting-place of the Hans Town merchants. It was destroyed in the Great Fire in 1665.

soon follows—to Oxford Kate's,[1] a curious tavern to choose,
which cost him 5s. Then there were purchases of various
articles of clothing and adornment, including ribbons for
his hat, 5s., and supporters for his linen tops, 7d. A day
or two later Johnson went across the Thames, paying a
waterman 1s. to take him there and back, to hire a coach to
go to Hemsted, in Kent. The following morning Francis paid
"a pair of oars", 1s., to row him over to the Surrey side[2]
again, for the famous George Inn[3] at Southwark, where—
together with Smyth—he took the appointed coach, not a
very expensive matter, down to Tonbridge. He continued
his journey on horseback to Hemsted, some considerable
distance away, the ancient seat of the Guldefords, near
Benenden, where he made a brief stop to see the church.
His visit to the Guldefords, with whom Lady Throckmorton
had also gone to stay, was with the intention of being
present at a wedding there which, considering all the circumstances, and particularly that Coughton Court was in such
a state of disrepair—may have been that of his only sister,
Anne, to Edward Guldeford, the eldest son and heir to the
family estates, which marriage took place just at that time.
The Guldefords were connexions of the Monsons, who lived
at Kinnersley Manor, in the parish of Horley, a few miles
cross-country from Dorking, and it was on this occasion that
Francis first met the young lady, Anne Monson, who
eventually was to become his wife.

Sheldon had also arrived at Hemsted, and Jack Parsons
had been sent there to attend on Francis. They all returned
together to London, travelling by a night coach from
Tonbridge to Southwark. On arrival they were rowed across
to Westminster, where Francis's breakfast cost him 10d.

Details of Johnson's bill follow which evidence that
during most of this visit to London, Francis had entertained
his mother and Mrs Mordaunt of Turvey, both of whose

[1] Otherwise the Cock Tavern in Bow Street, then kept by a woman
called "Oxford Kate". If not already notorious, it was soon to
become very much so.

[2] Pepys, in 1665, had to get to Deptford, and "there being no oars
to carry me, I was forced to call a skuller".

[3] Close to the Tabard, the starting-place of Chaucer's pilgrims,
demolished in 1875.

expenses he paid, as also a fee to Dr John Wilby, of Shore-
ditch, who had attended him for some complaint or another.
On this occasion the visit had extended over a fortnight,
and Francis was now beginning to think of his return to
Cambridge. So, a week before starting, £1 was deposited
as "an earnest for Cambridge stage coach.[1] Finally, after
paying for the binding of a book, 3s., and buying 2 tennis
rackets, 6s. 6d., and some sugar and fruit and a box to
carry it in, they began the return journey on May 13th,
when it was found necessary to pay a further £2 for coach
hire, having hired the stage-coach to carry us upon an
unusual day, and having no passengers but our company.
The coachman that carried them both stages[2] was given 2s.,
a man that held the coach in a bad way had 6d., they paid
for beer on the way, 2d., and for 2 bottles of Francis ale[3] to
carry in the coach, 1s. This time they had dinner at Epping
and, as usual, stayed at Bishop's Stortford for the night,
dining at Newport the next afternoon.

One of the first payments made after their return to
Cambridge may be significant, with reference to what has
been already said as to the status of Francis whilst living
there, for Bagley is now described as *passing* as his tutor.
The actual item is: "Given to Mr Bagley that passed as my
master's tutor in Cambridge, £2". Beer gives place to
cider, and there is the first mention of lemons, 2d. each,
and a solitary reference to lemon beer,[4] 6d., during this
month of May. Someone also seems to have drunk a little
wormwood beer[5]; tennis and bowls were played and lost;
a Vergil cost 2s. 6d.; and Mr Day was again consulted and
paid 5s., for curing of my master's eye, with which treatment the purchase of some whey, 4d., was associated.

[1] In *Several proceedings of State Affairs in England, Scotland and
Ireland from Thursday 31st August, to Thursday the 7th September,*
1654, No. 258, is this advertisement: "A Stage Coach goes from the
Swan to Grayes Inn Lane end to Holburn to the Rose in Cambridge
every Monday, Wednesday, and Friday, for 10s., and from the Rose
in Cambridge every Tuesday, Thursday, and Saturday for 10s.
Letters and small packets are sent by them".
[2] The stages as already noted.
[3] Possibly franchise ale.
[4] Lemonado, later lemonade.
[5] Beer infused with wormwood.

Then a new suit and coat were supplied by Angier, this time costing some £7 in all.

Towards the end of the month 3s. 4d. was paid for the return of £20 in specie, entrusted to the carrier, which 40 pence evidences the then stabilized rate—2d. per £1— which could be charged for such a transaction.

Francis about this time rode over to Caxton, some 12 miles distant from Cambridge, "to see the house"[1]—there is no indication as to what house—where 2s. was given to Mr Christey's and Mr Scarlett's servants. A visit was also paid to the church there. The next day he went to another bear-baiting, again somewhere near Cambridge, and whilst there his tethered mare broke loose, 10d. being paid for the trespass thus committed. At the house where the bear-baiting was, and also to the bearherd, 1s. was given.

May, which had been a full month for Francis, closed with a visit from young Mr Neville of Audley End, whom he took to see King's Chapel, where he gave the keeper— styled thus on this occasion—6d., afterwards entertaining his guest to white wine and macaroons, 1s. 8d. Perhaps the pair of Spanish leather shoes, 4s., bought earlier that same day, marked the occasion. Other guests were received a few days afterwards, two of them being Dr Throckmorton and his wife, at which time a quart of white wine was bought. After being entertained they too were taken to King's Chapel. Another guest was Major-General Skippon's[2] son, whom Francis took out on a fishing expedition, paying 5s. for boat-hire, and 2s. 6d. for refreshments.

Boating, in connexion with which another "duck to hunt" cost 8d., was popular in this month of June, and there were also at least two visits to Clare Hall bowling-green where Francis lost, as he also did at tennis three times. There is one item for balls in the tennis courts, 1s., at Christ's, where apparently they could be purchased, or

[1] There is a tradition that William Caxton, the first English printer, was born at Caxton, and that it was also the birthplace of Matthew Paris, the St. Albans chronicler.

[2] Major-General Philip Skippon who had a very distinguished career, on the Cromwellian side, in the Great Civil War. Francis's guest was doubtless Luke Skippon, the second son, who had just matriculated at Trinity. (Venn, *op. cit.*, Pt. I, Vol. IV, p. 86).

CAMBRIDGE: KING'S COLLEGE CHAPEL *c.* 1690

(From Loggan's "Cantabrigia Illustrata")

perhaps hired, of an attendant. Claret and cinnamon and
lemons and cherries were all a natural accompaniment of
these expenses, and the weather being warm Francis
purchased six pairs of thread socks, 6s. 6d. One of the last
items this month was of £1 4s., for two pounds of Spanish
tobacco given to Thomas Salwey and his brother.

Towards the end of June, Francis, horses having been
hired, rode with Smyth to Welden, stopping at Huntingdon,
where he gave 4d. to the prisoners, and 6d. to the poor.
At Welden the bells were duly rung, the ringers receiving
2s. for their welcome. The stay there was a long one, and
it was not until the end of July that they returned to
Cambridge. Whilst at Welden Francis had been to Deene,
where he also played bowls, and gave 6d. to a tumbler that
did tricks.

Returning to Cambridge for a brief period, arrangements
were made for a course of fencing-lessons with one Watson
after the vacation. There was also some more rowing on
the river; further small losses at tennis and bowls; and a
dinner at Peterhouse, where the butler had 6d. for his
attention. Then, amongst other things, Francis had his
sword[1] scoured; his violin and its case—which together had
cost £2 15s.—were brought down from London by the
carrier, 1s. 6d.; and bought a copy of Rider's Dictionary,[2]
14s.

Towards the end of August he was off again, this time to
Weston, and to the Gerys at Bushmead Priory—where he
lost at cards, 12s. Thence on to far-off North Ashton[3] to
Lady Frances Neville's, for some days—from which place
he visited Mr Bushell's wells,[4] 2s.—and so to Buckingham,

[1] Worn at that period almost as a matter of fashion.
[2] John Rider (1562–1632), whose *Bibliotheca Scholastica*, an
elaborate English-Latin and Latin-English dictionary, was first
published in 1589. The last edition appeared in 1640.
[3] A picturesque stone village lying south of Deddington, and
some 15 miles north of Oxford.
[4] Thomas Bushell's famous wells were at Enstone, some five miles
from Chipping Norton, where his "wonderful Rock of Enstone" was
one of the sights of Oxfordshire at this time. Robert Plot gives
two illustrations of it in his *Oxfordshire* (1677). For a particularly
interesting reference, see H. A. Evans's *Highways and Byways in
Oxfordshire and the Cotswolds*, pp. 387–90. (1905).

whence he went to a race at Brackley[1] where he lost 5s. At Brackley he also went to a wedding.

He was back again at Cambridge on September 13th, his sixteenth birthday, evidently with one or two more visits to Stourbridge Fair also in mind. A feature of this birthday celebration was a venison pasty, which must have been a fairly large one, for it cost 8s., and the entertaining of certain strangers that did dine then with my master added 7s. to the modest expenses connected with the event. Other items about this time were for two barrels of oysters, 4s. 8d., to send to his mother at Weston, together with some herrings for her breakfast, 1s. He also supplied himself with a hat and hat-case, 18s., and a leather hat-case, 2s. 6d.

Again he took Lilley and his wife to the Fair, where he spent 6s. on fairings for them. That same day he paid Mr Angier the tailor's bill for another suit. The inclusive cost was £5 16s. 10d., the items being—their order is thus— 1¾ yards of cloth, £1 11s. 6d., canvas, 1s. 4d., 2 yards of spotted shag and 2 yards of pillow fustian, 10s. 8d., 2 yards of dyed linen for the hose,[2] 2s., silk pads and collar, 2s. 6d., tabby, 8s. 4d., 4 dozen gold and silver buttons and a waist-button, 9s., loop-lace, galloon, and pockets, 2s. 6d., 72 yards of ribbon at 8d. per yard, £2 8s., and 3 yards of ferret ribbon,[3] 3s. In addition a sum of 8s. was charged for making the suit.[4]

In October there was a good deal of coming and going between Weston and Cambridge, and in November and December Francis had many violin lessons. He then also had his coat-of-arms painted and framed at a cost of 4s. 6d. and bought a copy of Howell's Epistles,[5] 4s. 6d., an almanack[6] with clasps, and pencils and paper.

Other expenses at this time included several supplies of

---

[1] In Northamptonshire, and seven miles from Buckingham.
[2] For lining the breeches.
[3] A kind of narrow ribbon used for fastenings.
[4] Cf. the items (p. 34) of another suit bought shortly afterwards.
[5] James Howell (d. 1666), author of Epistolae Ho-elianae, mostly written when he was a prisoner in the Fleet, and published in 1655.
[6] There is no present evidence of the issue of any Cambridge Almanack between 1642 and 1661, after which Pond, Swan, and others, appeared again.

the usual lozenges, half a pound of hair-powder, 2s., camphor balls, an English Vergil, 3s., and—interesting to record— oranges, 3d., in December, an item repeated in January.

Francis again spent his Christmas at Cambridge, at which time he gave to the tailor's men for their Christmas-boxes, 1s. 6d., to the shoemaker's men, 1s., and Lilley's servants had 3s. amongst them. Shortly after Christmas he rode over to Bushmead Priory to stay with the Gerys—where, on his departure, the servants had 6s. 6d. Back at Cambridge he went out to dinner several times, and horses were hired on more than one occasion, when my master did ride forth to take the air.

In the second week in January, 1656-7, arrangements were again made for fencing-lessons, the fencer being paid 1s. a week, and fencing-sticks, 1s. 4d., were bought. Smyth also then delivered to Francis his quarter's allowance for his expenses at play and tennis, £2, a new and more dignified arrangement, now that he was growing up. On January 17th he gave to see a crocodile,[1] 4d., and also purchased a book of Exordiums of Orations,[2] 2s. 6d. Other items included one for dressing and lining a hat, 1s. 6d.; another for "mending of a gunne",[3] 1s. 8d.; and the month closed with an item of 10s. "given to the University Music that played all the winter nights".

On St Valentine's Day (February 14th) there was a payment of 3s. for gloves for my master's valentine,—another one follows later—and for almonds, 6d., their first appearance. A little later Mr Day was paid 2s. for staying of the rhume[4] that fell into my master's eyes; and 6d. was given to see the Italian that did cut glasses. Again a hat figures, this time for refreshing of his hat, 1s.

At the end of the month another suit was ordered, for which the account is given in full. This time it cost

[1] John Evelyn, in London, in October, 1684, went to see "a crocodile, brought from some of the West India Islands, resembling the Egyptian crocodile".
[2] As yet unidentified.
[3] Doubtless this was a leathern gun or bottell for carrying wine.
[4] Lady Paston, (op. cit. p. 71) writing to William Paston, in June, 1624, tells him that a box of juice of liquorice is being sent to him: "It will stay the rhume when tobacco will not. I hope to hear you still hate the very smell of tobacco".

£5 0s. 2d., the items being 1¾ yards of cloth at 18s. per yard,
£1 11s. 6d., 1 yard of canvas and 2 yards of pillow fustian,
5s. 10d., galloon, pads, and collar, 2s. 4d., dyed linen and
pockets, 3s., 17 yards of ribbon, 17s., tabby for the suit and
coat, 12s. 9d., ferret ribbon and hooks and eyes, 1s. 11d.,
silk for the suit and coat, 3s. 3d., buttons for the coat,[1]
9s., 2½ yards of spotted shag for the doublet, 6s. 4d., loop
lace and a waist-button, 1s. 2d., 18 silver buttons, 5s. 3d.,
and a neck-button for the coat, 10d.

Early in March Sheldon arrived at Cambridge, coming
from Moor Hall, and bringing with him a small trunk which
he had bought for Francis, 13s.   There was also a sum of 18s.
to be paid for gloves which had been given to one Mistress
Headley on February 14th, she being my master's valentine
this year.[2]   On March 18th Smyth paid 8d. for the carriage
of his montero[3] from London, and it cost 6s. 6d. to alter his
clothes to fit Jack Parsons.

This, his last term, Francis paid much attention to his
violin, his teacher being one Alexander, who was paid £3 for
lessons extending over four months.   He was now also
taking more dancing lessons—given by Lilley, his landlord,
who at times also instructed him in the violin—and had a
number of riding lessons.   He kept his nag at the Red
Lion Inn for six weeks, the horsemeat costing £1 17s. 6d.,
and when he came away he distributed 8s. 6d. to Lilley's
servants, celebrated the occasion with wine at parting, and

[1] Very few in comparison with the previous suit.

[2] Apparently, therefore, he had had two strings to his bow on this
St Valentine's day, which reminds one that Pepys of course knew
a good deal about this subject.   As an instance, on Sunday, February 14th, 1661, he notes: "My Valentine [Mrs Batten] had her fine
gloves on at church to-day that I did give her", and he was much
more generous on at least one other occasion, when he gave, on
St Valentine's day, 1665–6, a dozen pairs of gloves to gay Mrs Pierce,
who had come to his house "with my name [written on a card] in
her bosom for her Valentine".

[3] Montero or Buckinghamo.   "A close hood [or cape] wherewith
travellers preserve their faces and heads from frost-biting, and
weather-beating in winter". (Cotgrave). Lady Paston, (op. cit.,
p. 97) writing to William Paston on December 4th, 1626, says:
"I pray thee have a great care to keep thyself very warm, and put
somewhat about thy neck for thou art very much subject to pains
in thy throat, and if need be wear a cape—there can come no harm
in keeping warm".

had his sumpter-trunks—which had been repaired and filled with all his belongings—loaded on a horse by the groom. Then, on March 20th, accompanied by Smyth and Parsons, he said goodbye to Cambridge and to all that it had meant to him, and Weston once again welcomed him home late that early spring evening.

He had left his fencing-sticks behind him, which it cost 6d. to return to him later on by the local carrier; also, purposely, the great trunk, the transport of which Angier, the tailor, took in hand, and paid 2s. 6d. for cords, and for mats to protect it in its transit to Weston. In it he packed another suit which he had made for Francis, at a cost of £6 12s., charging an additional 17s. for ribbon to make up the trimmings, and 1s. for a box for the suit.

The only evidence that Francis ever returned to Cambridge after those many happy days in 1654–57, is to be found in Professor Marjorie H. Nicholson's "Conway Letters", (1930), being the correspondence of Anne, Viscountess Conway, Henry More (Platonist and Fellow of Christ's College), and their friends, between 1642 and 1684. More, writing from Christ's on July 14th, 1671, to Lady Conway, says: "Sir Francis Frogmorton, who kept with us in our Hall this commencement, told me of the noble funeral of my Lady Dowager". This was Lady Frances Conway, who had been buried at Arrow, a few miles from Coughton, on the previous June 16th, at which ceremony Francis would seem to have been present. Incidentally it is of interest to note that More should spell his surname as Frogmorton, for "Frog" has been the family nickname for generations—perhaps indeed Francis may have been known by it at Cambridge—and much later on it was certainly used by Cowper, the poet, in his correspondence during his close friendship with the Throckmortons—"Mr. and Mrs. Frog", thus he styled them,—of his day, at Weston.

NOTE.—Since this book was first published a very interesting suggestion concerning Lilley's identity has been made, by Mr. G. de Fraine (Cambridge), in *Notes and Queries*, August 7th, 1948, pp. 339—40; see also Venn, *op. cit.*, Pt. I, Vol. III, p. 85, *sub* John Lilly (1663), son of John Lilly, musician, Cambridge.

Chapter III

OXFORD, LONDON AND THE COUNTRY, APRIL, 1658—APRIL, 1659

Those three years at Cambridge had doubtless passed all too quickly, and Francis was now back at Weston, his expenses there for some weeks, until well after Easter, being mostly concerned with his diet and his horses. Other expenses in April, 1658, were on a small scale, and included 2s. "given at the cook's with",[1] for carriage of a cloak bag[2] from Cambridge to Weston, 1s. 6d., and for carriage of my master's new suit and boots from Cambridge to Weston, 2s. For this suit there had also been 12 yards of ribbon to trim it, 8s. Mrs Guldeford—Edward Guldeford's bride—was also at Weston at this time, with her husband, and they went with her brother, Francis, to Newport Pagnell and to the Fortescues at Salden, where 2s. 6d. was given to the music, and the same sum to the servants. At Weston, 2s. 6d. was given at several times in the church when my master went to ring.

In mid-May Francis was off once more, this time with his mother,[3] into Warwickshire, Coughton being the main objective, where—amongst others—he stayed with his co-guardian Thomas Sheldon, at Moor Hall, who had had his watch and alarum mended for him—8s. this time—and brought him a pair of tweezers, £1, at Birmingham; rang the bells at Coughton; and bought a girdle and points,[4] and a pair of riding boot-hose, 12s., together with a pair of crimson silk stockings, £1 at Alcester, where he gave 2s. to the music, which he also did at Salden and elsewhere during this month. Whilst staying at Moor Hall—where the local morris-dancers performed before him and were well rewarded,

---

[1] Or withy, the willow wand or garland carried ceremoniously into the house at Easter by the cook, a custom which obtained at some country houses at that time. See also p. 56.

[2] A bag for his cloak or other clothes.

[3] Lady Throckmorton had now been a widow for nearly seven years, and was still only in her forties. It was about this time that she married Lewis Mordaunt.

[4] Laces with tagged ends, for tying.

6s.—he naturally saw a good deal of Sheldon and visited a number of other friends thereabouts. Some of them may have been invited to Coughton on June 13th, on which day Smyth notes the payment of 1s. to a man that did wade to beat up the ducks, when my master did duck-hunt in Coughton park ponds.

At Moor Hall, the joiner for mending the shovel-board was paid 1s., and another set of nine-pins, 1s.—this time called ninepegs—was bought evidently also for Francis's recreation whilst staying there.

Towards the end of June, accompanied by his mother, he paid two visits to Lady Carington at Wootton Wawen; and at Richard Kempson's at Oversley Lodge, near Alcester, he dined with Lord Shrewsbury,[1] the servants receiving 6s. Then there was another brief shopping visit to Alcester, where amongst other things an ounce of tartar, 8d., and more diapalma were purchased, and also a greatly additional supply of ribbon, 15s. 8d., with which to trim my master's suit. A sum of 4d. was also expended there for pictures, possibly prints of sacred subjects, or concerned with that forthcoming pilgrimage—though doubtless it was not thus spoken of outside the family circle—which was evidently contemplated either to Malvern Wells[2] or to the more famous St Winifred's Well[3] at Holywell, near Wrexham, in Flintshire, both reputed to be very efficacious for weak eyes, with which it has already been evident that Francis was somewhat troubled.

Thus Smyth set off for Worcestershire, and so to Malvern Wells to make enquiries, and on his return to Coughton it was decided not to go there, but to make the long journey to Wrexham for which, although recusants, they do not appear to have had passes. The horses were shod, the saddles re-stuffed, and Francis and Sheldon together set off along the bad roads which led thither, under a hot July sun. Their total expenses amounted to £7 9s. 5d., and unfortunately that is all the information that is deducible

[1] Who had lately succeeded to the earldom.
[2] Evelyn had been there on August 1st, 1654.
[3] Its curious story is told in the Golden Legend, published in 1512.

concerning this first pilgrimage to Holywell.[1] A week after his return to Coughton, Francis, with Smyth, went to stay with the Fortescues[2] at Cookhill, not many miles from Alcester, and then went on to Throckmorton, where there was music, 5s. at Thomas Salwey's, and the servants were given 12s. 6d. On their return they went to Hewell, near Bromsgrove, to see Lord Windsor, who drove Francis back to Coughton—no great distance away—in the coach, the mare being lame.

At this time Smyth paid £6 8s 8d. to Lewis Mordaunt—who had come to Coughton Court for a brief visit—for a runlet[3] of sack Francis had presented to Mrs Mordaunt as some return for her hospitality some months before; several briefs[4] for fire received 3s.; Lady Throckmorton was repaid £2 for holland which she bought to make my master's shirts; and Mr Throckmorton for two pairs of shoes which he bought for him in London, 9s.

During this stay at Coughton, Francis called on several of the tenants, among them being William Dewes, the son of a former tenant of Moor Hall, and described as a grazier, who in 1651 had been under suspicion as a Royalist.[5] He also entertained Francis on several later occasions.

August was well advanced before Francis was off again for Weston, after staying for a day or two at Moor Hall—where the servants received 15s.—and at the inn at Southam—half-way between Leamington and Daventry—for the night, my master and Mrs Mordaunt being then going to Weston. On the way to Southam they had briefly stopped at Budbrooke, near Warwick, the home of the Dormers,

---

[1] He went to Holywell again in August, 1658, the items for which visit are more detailed (v. pp. 47–8). The well is still, of course, visited by many pilgrims.

[2] Connected with the Fortescues of Salden, co. Buckingham and the Wyntours of Huddington Court, co. Worcester.

[3] Of at least several gallons.

[4] Royal Letters Patent, authorising collections for charitable purposes within churches, and sometimes from house to house.

[5] Information had been laid against him that he had held intelligence with the King's party in 1643, and had bought plundered goods, and conveyed them to the garrisons of Worcester, Evesham, Oxford, etc., for which he bought a protection from Prince Maurice and Colonel Knotsford. (*Committee for Advance of Money*, Pt. III, p. 1423).

where, as on their arrival at Weston, they were received with much ringing of the church bells. Smyth also reached Weston about this time, and shortly afterwards, when a saddle had been stuffed and chamered[1] for him, he set off for London to make arrangements for the forthcoming visit there, returning to Weston almost at once. Meanwhile Francis went over to Turvey to see some horses—where he gave 1s. to the keeper of Turvey park, and another to Mr Digby's[2] groom, from Gayhurst, close to Newport Pagnell —and to Tyringham, where he called on his friend, Francis Tyringham.

Early in September, Francis quitted Weston accompanied by Smyth and spent a few days in London, some 57 miles distant,—stopping for the night at Dunstable on the way there—before going into Surrey. Whilst in London he made a number of small purchases, and amongst other things had his sword scoured, for which he bought a new scabbard, and provided himself with a false scabbard, 4s. He also hired a hackney-coach one morning and went to Gray's Inn Fields, where the gatekeeper was paid 4d.

The journey into Surrey began at Lambeth, Francis having been rowed across the Thames, 1s., and there met by Smyth and a porter that went with the horses to Lambeth, for which he was paid 1s. On the way they stopped at Nonsuch House,[3] near Epsom, some ten miles from Lambeth, for an hour or so, and then went on to one Mrs Peaslie's. There is no direct evidence as to where she lived, but it would seem to have been at or near Dorking. She boarded them for rather more than 10 weeks, at £1 10s. a week for the two, they paying for their washing, horsemeat, etc.

On arrival there, Francis was joined by Sheldon, and the indispensable Jack Parsons rode over from Weston to

[1] Chamfered.

[2] John Digby of Gayhurst House, which had played its small part in the Gunpowder Plot. He was a brother of Kenelm Digby, killed at St Neots, co. Huntingdon, fighting for the King, July 9th, 1648. John Digby succeeded at Gayhurst in 1665, after the death of his exiled father, Sir Kenelm Digby.

[3] In the parish of Cuddington, see V.C.H., *Surrey*, III, 268–70, with illustrations. Henry VIII pulled down the church, the old manor house and the village, in order to make the site suitable for the erection of this costly building, which was never completed.

be in attendance on his master. Whilst in these Surrey
parts, Francis seems to have done a great deal of riding, and
paid 5s. 6d. for an iron bar to secure the stable door at
Mrs Peaslie's, where he was keeping at least three horses.
During this time he called on several people in the neigh-
bourhood, including John Evelyn the diarist, at Wootton,
3 miles from Dorking, and also Sir Richard Lashford and
Lady Diana Curson,[1] and there is an item of money to my
lady Curson's coachman that assisted Parsons in looking
to his horses. Eventually, deep in November, they all left
Mrs Peaslie's—her servants receiving 13s. 6d. amongst them
—and the horses were sent back to Weston, Francis and
Smyth returning to London by coach.

It was dark when they arrived at the George Inn, and
they had to hire a link porter, 9d., who lighted them out
of Southwark to the Old Exchange.[2] There, after some
refreshment—including cock ale—they hired a hackney-
coach, 5s., and porterage was paid for the trunks from
Arundel House[3] to their lodging, and to the porter there
that took charge of them. The next day more cock ale was
drunk, and Francis did some shopping, his purchases
including a half-shirt,[4] £1 4s., a band and cuffs, 4s., 2 pairs
of shoes, 8s. 6d., jessamy-butter,[5] 1s., a hone, 4s., and there
was some grinding of razors, 6d.

This stay in London was very brief. It included a
supper, with wine and ale, given to Sir Edward and Lady
Fortescue of Salden, and another visit to Gray's Inn Fields.
Parsons was sent on to Weston with the trunks, going by
the carrier's wagon, at a total expense of 19s. 2d., and Francis
and Sheldon then rode down there together, Smyth having
preceded them the previous day.

[1] The Cursons had intermarried with the Dormers, and were of
Waterperry, co. Oxford.

[2] Or Old Change, where a few years later Pepys had very good
cheer at an eighteenpenny ordinary, with singing and music, and
drank a good deal of wine.

[3] In the Strand, and at that time well-known as a setting-down
place.

[4] A sort of shirt-front. On October 13th, 1661, Pepys left off
half-shirts, and put on a waistcoat.

[5] An ointment perfumed with jasmine, of which the use was considered rather foppish at that time.

Under December 3rd there is an item of 2s. 6d. given to the brewer[1] on St Catharine's night,[2] (November 25th), at Weston. After a few days there, Francis was off again, this time to Henwick, in the parish of Thatcham, Berkshire, where he stayed for a fortnight with the Winchcombes, and then back to Weston, by way of Northampton, where the party—consisting of himself, John Mordaunt, another friend, and three servants—stayed the night, their expenses being £1 3s., with 4s. spent at Brackley the next day. On December 19th, 3 ozs. of syrup of althea[3] and 1 oz. of aloes, 2s. 7d., nerve oil and iris roots, 9d., and ingredients for the plaster and fistula water, 2s. 4d., were supplied, all for Francis. Christmas was spent at Lady Frances Neville's house at North Aston,[4] where Francis gave 1s. 6d. to the music and the mummers, and made other small gifts then and at the New Year.

Oxford now makes its first appearance in the accounts, under January 13th, 1657–8, on which day Smyth arrived there from North Aston, to take lodgings for my master, who had moved from Lady Neville's. Sheldon and Salwey had been paying another brief visit to the Dormers at Budbrooke, and it is quite possible that while they were there it had been decided that Francis should now also have some experience of academic life at Oxford. However, his health was unsatisfactory during most of the winter, which may have accounted for the fact that he did not go to Oxford

[1] The brewer of the Catharine bowl.

[2] John Brand, in his *Popular Antiquities of Great Britain*, (1853), notes an interesting annual observance of this day, which had existed at Worcester "until within a very recent period" by the Dean and Chapter of Worcester. It was the last day of their general audit, when they distributed amongst the inhabitants of the college precincts a rich compound of wine, spices, etc., specially prepared for the occasions, and called the Catharine or Cattern bowl. Amongst other Worcestershire instances of the observance of this day is one noted by Jabez Allies, in his *Antiquities and Folk-Lore of Worcestershire*, (1852).

[3] Marsh mallow.

[4] When the church at Steeple Aston, close to North Aston, was restored in 1842, "the panelling of the Lady Chapel came from a manor-house of the Throckmorton family in Worcestershire, probably Harvington Hall". Rev. C. C. Brookes, *History of Steeple Aston and Middle Aston*, (1929), p. 225.

until the middle of March. His long stay at North Aston terminated on February 14th, at which time he started on his journey to Weston, where there was much to be done for him after his absence from home, including the making of shirts and waistcoats, a supply of laces for his waistcoats, the mending of the heels of his shoes, and the buying of hair-powder, and also of a pair of crimson cotton stockings, 8s., given to him by his mother.   Coal for fire for his chamber at Weston—24 cwt. for £2—was obtained, and also a good supply of candles—24 lbs. for 6s.

The ride to Weston was broken for the night at Buckingham—where Francis and Smyth were joined by Lewis Mordaunt. The next day they all went on to Weston where physic for my master by the appointment of Dr Medford—whose fee for attendance was £1—was ordered, together with 6 ozs. of lozenges, from Mr Day at Cambridge.

At Weston, where he had been welcomed with the usual church bell-ringing Francis was soon well enough to visit several of his immediate neighbours. Then early in March he went back to North Aston for a brief stay, and eventually, on the 16th, he and his little retinue alighted at the inn at Oxford, when my master first went to study there, where the expenses amounted to 19s.   That same day he bought 2 pairs of shoes, a pair of pumps[1] and a pair of slippers, at a total cost of 14s. 6d., and also 1 lb. of sugar, 1s.

The next day Francis went to a tailor—not named— where 5 yards of cloth for my master's suit and cloak, at 22s. per yard, cost £5 10s., and silk and tabby for the lining, "cloth for the stockings", and buttons, together added £2 14s. to that amount. In the afternoon he, with Smyth, visited several of the schools and colleges, which entailed half-a-guinea in gratuities.

It now transpires that the inn at which they had alighted was the famous Mitre, where the horsemeat cost 3s. 6d., but the next day they moved into rooms—Mrs Holway's— where they paid £1 10s. a week for their diet. One of the next things to be purchased was a load of wood for the fires, 17s. 8d., and there was further expense for the suit, for

---

[1] "Pumpes are shooes with single soles and no heels", 1688. Randle Holme, *Armoury*, Vol. III, p. 142 (*O.E.D.*).

OXFORD: STREET LIFE IN 1675

(*From Loggan's "Oxonia Illustrata"*)

which 20 yards of ribbon[1] and 28 yards of silver twist to trim it, were considered necessary and cost £1 16s. 4d. As the making of the suit, cloak, and stockings came to 16s., the total cost of this first—and last—Oxford outfit was £10 16s. 4d.

Other purchases in those early Oxford days, destined indeed to be so brief, included some holland with which to make my master's bands—otherwise his collars and his cuffs—a pair of silk tops, 10s. 6d., paper and sealing-wax, 1s. 2d., and more lozenges, 1s. 6d.; and this time the mending his watch, which often required attention, cost 5s. 6d.

Then there was a payment of £1 to the dancing-master for entrance, and two visits to the barber, 3s. Two days later Francis and Smyth again went sight-seeing, this time to several libraries and chapels of colleges, 6s. 6d.; and £1 was paid as a fee for entrance to the music-master, together with the purchase of a music-book, 1s. 8d. Among other expenses incurred during the next week were those for a new blade and sheath for my master's sorry shell haft, hair-powder, a ribbon for his wig, a paper-book, buckles, and leathers[2] for his stockings, a table[3] to set down the linen that was sent to be washed, another girdle and points, and a pair of flems[4] for the groom.

A few days later there happened an unfortunate accident which evidently contributed to bringing these Oxford days to an abrupt conclusion. Francis, together with two others for whom he had hired horses,[5] had ridden out into the country, to a Mr Berry's, where he dined. On the way back he fell off his horse—of course a not uncommon happening along those then wretched and cavernous roads—and, evidently never much good on horseback, he must have sustained some injury. So, on returning to Oxford, Dr Clayton was called in, and also the chirurgeon and his man, their total fees being £2 12s. 6d. The apothecary for physic

---

[1] On April 27th, 1660, Pepys, aboard ship, notes: "This morning, Pim [the tailor] spent in my cabin, putting a great many ribbons to a suit".

[2] Presumably leggings.

[3] Tablet.

[4] Farrier's lancets.

[5] He himself kept two horses whilst at Oxford, as he had also done in his later days at Cambridge.

charged 12s.; two days later the doctor had another 10s., for a fee; and a tincture, by Dr Clayton's prescription, cost 3s. 6d. That same day 6d. was paid for a dramatic play-book, bought for the invalid's recreation during his enforced inactivity, which however does not appear to have been of long duration.

At the end of March, having settled their weekly accounts, which included the carriage of his hat from London, 1s., and one pound of loaf sugar, 1s. 3d., they paid a visit to Wadham College and St John's College, 2s. 6d. A week later, evidently acting under the doctor's advice, Francis together with Smyth and the two servants went into the country, Smyth having paid a bill at the Mitre. The horses were led out of the town by a man who received 6d. for his trouble.

This visit of convalescence was made to Mr Sheldon's of Weston, that is to say to old Weston House, in the parish of Long Compton, Warwickshire, some 24 miles from Oxford, where at this time William Sheldon, the father of "The Great Sheldon" (Ralph Sheldon), was living. He was a cousin of Francis's Thomas Sheldon.

They then went on to Wootton Wawen, where Francis was the paying guest of his aunt Lady Carington. She was by no means a wealthy woman, and he had three servants with him, but the charges for all of them for their diet for 2 weeks only amounted to £2 12s. Lady Carington had formerly lived at Ledwell Park, near Oxford, but her husband—Sir Charles, also a devoted Roman Catholic—became obliged to remain abroad during the greater part of the Protectorate, as residence in England had been made so difficult for him. At this juncture it is of interest to note that Francis, at Oxford a little later on, loyally erected the monument still to be seen in Christchurch Cathedral, to commemorate his uncle—on the Carington side—Sir John Smith[1] who had been knighted at Edgehill and, after a renowned career, fell, mortally wounded, fighting for his king at Bramdean, in Hampshire, on March 29th, 1644. He was buried in the Cathedral three days later.

---

[1] *Wootton Wawen: Its History and Records*, (1936) by W. Cooper, pp. 31–2, with portrait.

The stay at Wootton was short, and Francis, with his servants, was soon on his way back to Oxford. They stopped a night at Chipping Norton, taking the road again the next morning for Woodstock, where Francis, falling of his ague there, was obliged to stop for the night at one of the inns, the expenses there being £1 2s. It was evidently quite impossible for him to ride on, so the horses were led back to Oxford, some seven miles distant. No coach was procurable at Woodstock, so one had to be sent out from Oxford, the bait at Woodstock costing 1s. 6d. and the hire of the coach 13s. With them they took a pint of wine and a bottle to carry in the coach, 1s. 2d. in all. The fit of ague had also necessitated the summoning of Dr Clayton and the apothecary to Woodstock, for which this time a total fee of £1 10s. was paid, and when Francis reached Oxford— returning to the rooms at Mrs Holway's—Clayton paid him a second visit, 10s.

It was now April 1658, during which month preserved damsons, 1s. and oranges, 1s. 2d., come into the accounts, and a load of wood for the fires cost 17s. 6d. A few days later the doctor was paid a further and comparatively large fee of £3, and the apothecary for physic, £1 8s.

However, early in May, Francis was able to pay a visit to Brasenose College. He also had a fine coat made, for which he purchased 3½ dozen silver buttons, 10s. 6d., some ribbons for the sleeves of the coat, 3s., and some silver twist and silk, 4s. Amongst other payments at this time were: to the dancing-master for one month, £1; for teaching of my master to play on the violin, 3 weeks, 15s.; for a pair of Spanish shoes, 4s.; and to the apothecary for a julep—an expensive one too—8s.

This was the close of the Oxford days, so brief and so differently lived to those at Cambridge. On May 9th, 1658, there was a final settlement with Mrs Holway, and Francis and his servants set off again for Wootton Wawen, the coach-hire costing £3 17s. 6d., with 17s. 6d. for expenses on the journey, and 10d. for 2 bottles for the indispensable juleps. Before leaving Oxford, he also bought a pair of pearl silk stockings, £1 4s., and also another pair of thread stirrup-stockings to take away with him. Then a new hilt and scabbard for his sword, together with a hood for the hilt, were purchased, the whole costing £1 9s.; the ribbons on his suit were turned; some new shirts were bought; and he took with him a very plentiful supply of hair-powder. He had not yet recovered from his accident, and had to have a nurse whilst at Wootton, during which month or so there was music at times. At this time it is evident that the builders were busy at Moor Hall, which Smyth went over to see, and had to be guided over the ford; and wood was sent over from Coughton for the fires in Francis's chamber, he still being the paying guest at Wootton.

Towards the end of the month—it seems to have been a cold May—Francis was able to take to the road once again, and doubtless was very ready to do so, especially at such a time of year. So to Coughton Court and to Throckmorton he went for a short stay, where at both places he was welcomed by the ringing of the church bells, and both bands of ringers had 5s. to share amongst them, the few old almswomen at Coughton being given 1s. for their humble welcome.

Back at Wootton again a sum of 16s. 10d. was incurred when, on June 21st, John Throckmorton, an uncle of Francis, was paid a bill of expenses at Stratford—the only time that Stratford-on-Avon appears in these accounts—when Francis brought young Charles Carington and his lady towards London. Smyth was also now ill, as is evidenced by the payment of 10s., "for James Waters's[1] diet for 2 weeks being with my master in my sickness". Shortly afterwards Francis again went to see Sheldon at Moor Hall, where there was music, and the servants had 4s. 6d. amongst them, and he also paid visits to James Waters's home—where he dined —and to other houses in the district, including that of Sir Charles Lee, who makes more than one appearance in these affairs.

At this time Francis supplied Jack Parsons with a barber's apron, 2s. 6d., for use when he shaved him, and other purchases included a pair of Spanish leather shoes, 4s., a pair of doe-skin gloves, 2s. 6d., tabby for lining his doublet and

[1] The Waters family had lived at Moor Hall before Thomas Sheldon became the tenant.

opening of the sleeves, and yet another girdle and two
points, 12 yards of ribbon to make black cuffs, 10 sets of
buttons for handkerchiefs,[1] 2s., and more hair-powder.
Soon afterwards Smyth rode into Gloucestershire, to Chipping Campden Fair to buy a horse, and returned with a brown
nag known as Flavel, £7.

This was early in August, 1658, and there was a second
pilgrimage to Holywell now pending, which would seem to
imply that the first one—in July 1657—had been deemed
efficacious.   On August 11th Francis, and Lord Shrewsbury,[2]
who had been staying with him at Coughton Court, again
dined with Richard Kempson, and the next day Francis
and Smyth set off to ride to Birmingham, where they bought
two pairs of spurs, 2s., and so on to Wolverhampton, where
the first night was spent.   Here an inkhorn, 6d., and
1 lb. of sugar[3] to carry on the journey, 1s. 2d., were bought.
They then went on to Newport in Shropshire, the party
now consisting of Francis, Ambrose Throckmorton[4] and
his man, a Mr Harcourt, and two servants.   There they all
stayed for the night.

The next stage was to Whitchurch, where they slept at
the inn, and had supper and breakfast, 10s. 8d., and so on
to Chester, with beer on the road, and the purchase of
another pound of sugar, 1s. 4d.   Arrived there, they
alighted at another unnamed inn, which did not please
them, so they went on to a better one, where they supped,
had music, and slept.   The next day was Sunday, and
Francis and his friends dined at 1s. each, the servants
having a dinner which cost 6d. each.   Beer that day cost

---

[1] Small handkerchiefs, some 3 or 4 inches square, with a button at
each corner, appear to have been somewhat fashionable just then.
See also p. 61.

[2] The Earl of Shrewsbury, who had succeeded to that title in
February, 1654–5, a staunch Cavalier.   He married Anna Maria,
daughter of Robert (Brudenell), 2nd Earl of Cardigan.   Lord
Shrewsbury died in London on March 16th, 1667–8, at Arundel
House, of wounds received in a duel with the Duke of Buckingham,
the paramour of his infamous wife (v. Pepys, Diary, January 17th,
1667–8).

[3] It may have been bought to sweeten the wine which they drank
on their way.

[4] Ambrose Throckmorton, another uncle.

2s., and white wine only 5d. The party rode on to Holywell after their meal, where later they had supper and more beer; with strong waters for Ambrose Throckmorton, 4d. Here there was also music, and a pint of sack and a quart of burnt wine[1] cost 2s. 5d. The poor there, 5s. 6d., certainly came off very well in comparison with other places where Francis had always remembered them, but then these other places were not comparable with the shrine of St Winifred of Holywell, to which they went the next day, and which was always particularly infested with beggars. This happened to be August 15th, the Feast of the Assumption of Our Lady, and was possibly selected with intention. Here the woman that kept the chapel was given 1s. 6d.; 5s. 8d. was paid for more burnt wine when they went into the well; and 1s. 6d. for moss[2] and stones and to the man that kept clean about the well. The visit to the well was repeated the next day, after which the party returned by the same way that they had come, Francis buying yet more sugar to carry home as they passed through Wrexham.

On reaching Coughton, Francis heard of the death of his friend, Henry Mordaunt. There is no evidence as to where he was buried—it cannot have been very far away from there, probably at Walton—and Francis at once went into mourning for him. So a pair of mourning shoes for him and a pair for Jack Parsons, cost 6s. 6d., Jack's stockings being 3s. The actual making of all my master's mourning for Mr Mordaunt cost £1 16s., his pair of black silk stockings, £1 4s., and one pair of his gloves was dyed black for him. At this time a prayer-book also cost 6s., but of course it may not have had anything to do with the funeral; three saddles

---

[1] Heated wine, see Lady Paston's reference to burnt sack, p. 24, n. 2.

[2] Doubtless the moss and stones were brought back to Weston, where Cowper also had his moss-house some 150 years later. Pennant, in his *Tours in Wales* (ed. 1883), Vol. I, pp. 40–55, with illustration of the well, says: The waters [of St Winifred's Well] are indisputably endowed with every good quality attendant on cold baths . . . Some eminent botanists have reduced the sweet moss and the bloody stains [on the stones] to mere vegetable productions, far from being peculiar to our fountains". See also T. Deloney, *The Pleasant and Princely History of the Gentle-Craft: (c.* 1675), p. 3; *Gentleman's Magazine,* August, 1804; Joan Parkes, *Travels in the 17th Century,* (1925), pp. 245–6.

Engraved by Angus, from a Drawing for the Gallery of Nature & Art.

HOLYWELL: ST. WINIFRED'S WELL IN 1821

were covered for mourning, 4s.; a black bridle and stirrup leathers cost 2s. 6d., a pair of black spurs, 1s., and the tailor's man that brought home the mourning, from Alcester, was given one shilling. The making of Jack's suit and coat cost 7s.

The next day the three rode off to the funeral, for which Smyth did not need any mourning, except for his saddle to be covered with black cloth, as already shown, for he had recently attended the funeral of a relative. The last mention of this matter was the gift of 2s. 6d. to James, Mr Mordaunt's man, when he delivered to Francis Mr Mordaunt's case of razors, a curious memento of the deceased, but doubtless a useful one.

Francis's eighteenth birthday was now at hand, so against it Smyth bought 10 quarts and 1 pint of claret and 1 quart of sack, all—apparently but incredibly—for 11s. 6d. A little later he paid for a sword and sword-belt for Francis £1 10s., also for a pair of riding-boots, 14s., and for treeing his boots, 3d.

During this stay at Moor Hall, Francis made various purchases at Alcester, and when he came away he distributed 16s. 6d. to the servants, before leaving for Weston once again. The first night was spent at Warwick, where the party consisted of himself, his mother, Dr Hernshaw,[1] George Gery,[2] and Richard Kempson, and two servants. The bill at their inn amounted to £2 18s., and the horsemeat came to 18s. 8d., which was unusually expensive, but in this case certainly included the actual stabling of the horses. The next day, Francis, his mother and the servants supped, slept and breakfasted at Daintry—Daventry—and went on to Budbrooke, where they stayed that night. Ultimately they reached Weston, Smyth having remembered the poor on several occasions—by order from my master and my lady —as they passed along the road, and also having made a small contribution to a brief for fire. The items concerning this Moor Hall visit come to an end with one of £3 paid to the carters that brought the many travelling-trunks thence

[1] Of Alcester.

[2] Of Bushmead Priory. He had been taken prisoner at Naseby in 1645.

to Weston. At this time the first large amount is noted in the accounts when Smyth, without giving any details, "delivered to my lady by the command of my master, for which I have their receipts", £81 10s. 4d.

Evidently a change had now come over the spirit of young Francis's dreams, and it all seems to have begun with that visit to Hemsted, for not long after he returned to Weston a velvet coat was sent down from London, together with a sword belt with silver buckles, £3 8s., more jessamy-butter, 2s., a hawking bag, 1s. 6d., a tortoiseshell comb and case, 2s. 6d., and a hood for my master's nag, 2s., which were some other items of the moment. Then Smyth was despatched definitely to Dorking—he being out six days, and his expenses £1 10s. 6d. From Dorking he sent a messenger to Kinnersley Manor, already mentioned, and the next day Smyth, who for some undiscoverable reason had been appointed this emissary of Francis's offer of marriage, went there and duly tendered it to Anne Monson. The offer was accepted, and Smyth was accordingly entrusted with all the arrangements for Anne[1] and her widowed mother to meet Francis and his mother in London.

Meanwhile Francis himself had been coursing with James Lowe[2]—not a very desirable acquaintance—at Clifton Reynes, and had also accompanied him to Wellingborough, where he entertained him to dinner, together with Dr Hernshaw. After Smyth's return to Weston, bearing the good news, doubtless already anticipated, from Kinnersley Manor, he—on horseback and with two grooms also in attendance—escorted Francis and his mother, with her lady's maid, to London by way of Newport Pagnell, in the old family-coach drawn by four horses, the first stage being

---

[1] Daughter and sole heiress of John Monson, son of Sir William Monson, Vice Admiral of England, temp. James I., v. V.C.H., *Surrey*, Vol. III, p. 203. In 1827, when old Weston House was practically demolished, a number of family portraits were removed to Coughton Court, amongst them being one of her, painted when she was Lady Throckmorton. (Lipscomb, *op. cit.*, Vol. IV, p. 403).

[2] James Lowe lived at Clifton Reynes, quite close to Olney, to which he had succeeded in 1657. He is said to have been extravagant and litigious, and about the year 1672 was obliged to sell his estate, after which little else is known of him. He died in 1683, and was buried in the family vault in Clifton Church.

to the inn at Market Street,[1] where the expenses for this party of six came to £3 17s. 4d. The second stage was the short one to High Barnet, 16 miles from their destination, where the night at the inn cost only £2 2s. Francis's boots were made clean and staffed[2] at both inns on the road; money was given to the poor; and toll was paid at the gates in the fields in London.

On their arrival in London they went at once to the lodgings which had been taken for them, and Smyth bought candles and faggots for the first night, being that of November 3rd. Perhaps, all things considered, they could have done without music that evening, whether in or outside the house, but it just had to be, and the players were rewarded with 2s. 6d.

The next day Francis took a hackney-coach and went off to play several games of tennis, Smyth meanwhile depatching the grooms back to Weston, with the coach and all the horses, an account of £1 14s. having been paid for horsemeat, and for cleansing of the coach, and liquoring[3] it. Other items of expenditure that day included a primer,[4] 5s., a standish, 1s. 8d., paper and blacklead pencils,[5] 8d., 3 pairs of shoes and a pair of galloshooes,[6] 16s., and a little tobacco for my lady.[7] In addition, Lady Throckmorton was also supplied with syrup, 4s. 3d., by a neighbouring apothecary, and Francis was trimmed at his barber's, 2s. 6d.—where he bought his usual jessamy-butter—in preparation for the great and eagerly anticipated arrival of Anne Monson and her mother.

Some slight delay ensued, however, so there was more tennis and some considerable instruction at the fencing-school, and by one Isaac at the dancing-school; also at other

---

[1] Or Markyate Street, near Dunstable, and 29 miles from London.
[2] Treed, cf. p. 49.
[3] Oiling.
[4] Probably a devotional manual.
[5] Made wholly of lead.
[6] Galoshes.
[7] Instances of women smokers at this period are, of course, not uncommon.   Later on for instance, in 1697, a quarter of a pound of tobacco cost Sister Louisa, a married Quaker, 2½d. (v. the account-book kept by Sarah Fell, the step-daughter of the Quaker, Charles Fox; also *Memoirs of St. Simon*, Vol. I, p. 11).

times Francis went to Somerset House; to the Old Bailey on several occasions; to St Paul's Churchyard; and to Sir Charles Lee's town house, always taking a hackney-coach to get to his destination.

The Monson ladies now at last arrived in town and, during their first days there, Francis—the joyous occasion of the betrothal having evidently been bruited abroad— had to pay no less than three times for flourishes of trumpets with which the happy party was greeted. This distinction altogether cost him 10s., one of the payments indeed being for two companies of trumpets. At this time he also played and lost a little at cards, and Smyth paid for small ale at several times, 6d.; for 2 dozen of bottle ale[1]; for 3 bottles of cock ale and China ale,[2] 1s. 6d.; and, coincidentally, for The History of China,[3] 7s. The weather was cold and foggy, so 2 bushels of coal for my master's chamber, 2s. 1d., were obtained, and later on more coal 1s. 9d., and flannel for his drawers, 5s. 6d.; also Gibson, a tailor, supplied him with a stuff suit and coat and another velvet coat, £16.

England now faced those days of national uncertainty which came between the Protector's death and the Restoration. On November 26th, only four days after Cromwell's very imposing funeral,[4] Francis—albeit such a staunch young Royalist—could not resist a desire to go to Westminster

[1] Always thus styled in these accounts.

[2] There is another item of China ale, 1s. 4d., under July 5th, 1659, and later, for ale to make butter ale at several times, 1s. 6d. China ale and goat ale (p. 58) both require definition.

[3] Juan Gonzales de Mendoza's *History of the Kingdom of China*, first published in Spanish in Rome in 1585. Other editions and translations appeared as time went on, and a Latin version was published at Antwerp in 1655. An earlier edition had been published in English, a copy of which was probably what Francis purchased.

[4] The Protector had died of a tertian ague on September 3rd, and the expense of his funeral was enormous. A little more than two years later, Evelyn, writing under December 30th, 1660, says: "This day (O the stupendous and inscrutable judgments of God!) were the carcasses of those arch rebells Cromwell, Bradshaw the Judge who condemned his Majestie, and Ireton, sonne-in-law to the Usurper, dragg'd out of their superb tombes in Westminster among the Kinges, to Tyburne, and hang'd on the gallows there from 9 in the morning till 6 at night, and then buried under that fatal and ignominious monument in a deepe pit...." See also *Notes and Queries*, 2nd Series, Vol. XII, p. 146.

December.
1658

		li.	s.	d.
2.	For Cork hire	00.	02.	06
	Given att the opera for 8 persons	01.	04.	00.
	For Charges for my mrs Gould	00.	03.	06
	For Sugar	00.	01.	00
	paid to mrs Pate for my mrs & his 2 servants Diett for one weeke ending the 2 of Jober	01.	15.	00.
	To the poor	00.	00.	06
	for Core hire	00.	01.	00.
	Deliud to my mr att my Lord of Northamptons house to play att Cards	02.	11.	06
	For 2 doz: of bottle Ale & portadge of it	00.	07.	00
	for a banquett to entertaine mrs Monson	00.	07.	06
7	For Core hire	00.	01.	06.
	For a pair of winter bootes and a pair of Shooes	01.	03.	00
	For An Indian night Gowne	02.	13.	00.
	Exp. att ffrancis Drances house my mr mrs Gilliard and mrs Throats being there	00.	03.	00.
	Given then att the Tower in severall places	00.	05.	06
	For a pair of Kid mis Gloves	00.	06.	06
	Given to mr Crowder	00.	05.	00
	For porter: Lozenges for my mrs Gould	00.	02.	00.
	For sugar of Roses	00.	02.	00.
	For Core hire to the Tower & Exchange	00.	04.	06.
8o	For 2 Links	00.	00.	06
	Deliud to my mr	00.	05.	00
	For 6 bottels of Ale	00.	01.	06
	for a link	00.	00.	03
	Given to see the frentz mans shewe att mrs Monsons Lodgings	00.	00.	06
	For Core hire	00.	01.	06
	To a poor woman att mr Jremings request	00.	01.	00
	For a Riding band	00.	01.	10.
9	paid to mrs Pate for my mrs Diett & 2 servants for a weeke ending the 9th of November	01.	15.	00.
	For 4 strangers one meale	00.	04.	00.
	Given to mrs Pate 2 servants	00.	10.	00.
	To a poor woman	00.	00.	02
	For Cords for the trunk and boxe	00.	00.	10.
	For horsmeate & shooing & given to the Ostler	00.	12.	00
	To my Lady Dranes man	00.	02.	00
	To a poor gentn att mrs Cerces Request	00.	02.	06
	Exp. att St Albons where we baited	00.	09.	08.

	li.	s.	d.
The totall of this page is	16.	07.	09

PAGE FROM SMYTH'S LEDGER, DECEMBER, 1658

Abbey, to see the tombs and the Protector's monument, which cost him 2s. 6d. Despite the great funeral, London was certainly not dull, for on December 2nd Francis, although he had a cold, went with his party to the Opera, where he had taken seats, £1 4s., for 8 persons, and later that same evening played at cards at my Lord of Northampton's[1] house, for which purpose Smyth handed him £2 11s. 6d. About this time there was a banquet,[2] 7s. 6d., for Mrs. Monson, perhaps at Mulberry Garden.

Then followed the purchase of a pair of winter boots and a pair of shoes, £1 3s., a pair of riding gloves, 6s. 6d., and an Indian (silk) night-gown, cost £2 13s. Incidentally, too, Francis made another visit to the Tower, this time with the ladies, where he spent 5s. 6d. in several places, and to the Old Exchange, where he bought the usual lozenges, 2s., and some sugar of roses, 2s. On November 8th it was foggy, so he had to pay no less than three linkmen to light him on his way in a hackney-coach which he had hired to go to and from the Frenchman's show—thus—at Mrs Monson's lodgings, to which performance he gave 6d.

And now of course all too soon for Francis the happy little party must break up. The Monson ladies returned to Kinnersley Manor, and on December 9th Francis and his mother started off for Weston in a hired coach, the family coach having been sent back to Weston, and the trunks going by carrier's waggon. The horses were baited at St Albans, and the night was spent at that expensive inn at Market Street, which cost them £2 7s. 10d. The road on to Dunstable the next morning was either particularly bad, or there was snow or frost about, for 2s. 6d. had to be divided amongst 5 men that guided the coach down the hill at Dunstable.

Christmas came and went at Weston, but the only evidence of it is that Francis played and lost at shovel-board, and that on one occasion he had £1 11s. delivered

---

[1] A Royalist leader who, in September and October, 1659, at the time of Sir George Booth's attempted rising, was held a close prisoner in the Tower.

[2] At this period the use of the word banquet generally implies a dessert.

to him by Smyth for card-playing and, on another, 15s., for cards at Christmas. On December 20th, 2 lbs. of sugar were bought for his marmalade. The year closed—the unofficial close—with the usual distribution of New Year's gifts of money to various people. At this time Thomas Terry, the aforementioned steward at Weston, begins to figure more prominently in the accounts.

Early in January 1658–59, Francis rode to Northampton to meet his brother-in-law, Edward Guldeford, and Thomas Sheldon. There he purchased 3 ells of Holland for Hirthe caps,[1] 10s. 6d., an ell of holland for riding-bands, 9s. 6d., and buttons for those bands, 2s. On the 5th, back again at Weston, he gave to the fuel at Twelfthtide,[2] 1s. A later account shews that Greece, a haberdasher, whose shop he had visited whilst at Northampton, was paid for a round-crown hat, £1 4s., for a demicastor,[3] 4s., for a leather hat-case and padlock, 2s. 6d., for another demicastor and band, £1 15s., all the hats being sent to Weston, the box and porterage together costing 1s. 6d.

That same month Francis gave his sister, Mrs Guldeford, a dozen pairs of kid gloves, at 1s. 7d. per pair, and Mrs Thwaites—to whom he had already lost small sums at cards on several occasions—six pairs at the same price, bought at Olney, these being also New Year gifts. He now went off, with Terry, first to Buckingham, calling on the way at Major Harry Salwey's—one of the Stanford family—at Old Stratford.[4] At Buckingham, where they stayed the night, for horsemeat and at the inn £1 6s. was paid, and then they went on to Charlbury, in Oxfordshire, to see a horse, where they spent the second night, £1 6d. Returning the same way, they had dinner, 9s. 6d., at Buckingham,

---

[1] A sort of cap which still requires fuller definition.

[2] The fuel was probably for the large bonfire and the twelve small ones—symbolical of Our Lord and the Apostles, as lights of the world—which it was customary, at least in some counties, to light in the fields, on either the eve of Twelfth Day, or on Twelfth Day itself.

[3] A hat made of beaver's fur, or of other fur of poor quality.

[4] So called, on the presumption of superior antiquity, to distinguish it from Stony Stratford, co. Buckingham, from which it is separated by the River Ouse, over which is a bridge. (George Baker, *Northamptonshire*, I, 137).

during which Francis gave at the table to the relief of two poor men whom he had noticed as he arrived at the inn, 2s., his attention also being called to a poor gentleman to whom he gave 2s. 6d. The next day £1 was paid in boot between the bay nag and the grey mare, in connexion with which bargain John Digby's groom was given 1s. Indeed all these January days were more or less associated with horsy transactions, interspersed with a little card-playing— at which the stakes were beginning to increase—and a good deal of shovel-board.

Other items during the month included 2s. given to Digby's man when he gave my master 3 pheasants; £2 2s. given to Francis when he played cards, at Wellingborough, with Digby and James Lowe; 2s. to a man that pitched the bar at Digby's request, to display his strength; and 2s. 6d. to Mrs Franks to buy wax, for candle-making.

The outdoor conditions in the first part of February were bad, so during that period there were comparatively large losses—several guineas—at cards at Weston, one of the games being of gleek, played with John Throckmorton, and with Mrs Thwaites, who again won, and another of double-hand cribbage[1] at Tyringham, when Francis lost £1. Another loss was at cards and shovel-board, £1 18s. 6d.

A quiet time followed and it was not until late in March that Francis went far afield, this time his eventual destination once more being Moor Hall, where he spent a few days, and then went on to Throckmorton to stay with Salwey, taking some fish with him—it was in Lent—and being again welcomed by the bells. The journey to Moor Hall had been made with Mr Gery, of Bushmead Priory, who about this time purchased for him, in London, a copy of "Pointus Meditations",[2] £1 10s. On arrival Francis at once fell ill, being attended for ten days by Dr Hearnshaw, whose fees came to £5. Yarnold, the Alcester apothecary, supplied the necessary physic, 19s., his messenger being given 6d. for bringing a clyster[3] for Francis. On April 9th

---

[1] Four-handed cribbage.
[2] Pontanus, Ludovicus. *Meditations*. Translated by R. Gibbons, 1610.
[3] Injection (see *O.E.D.*).

the return to Weston was possible, but this time in the old Coughton Court family coach-and-four, two halts being made upon the way, one at Budbrooke and the other at Daventry.

A few days after reaching Weston Francis received a present of a white mare from his relative, Sir Thomas Smith, and shortly afterwards went to the horse race in the Chase—Yardley Chase—having been previously provided with money, and a money-wallet, 1s. 1d. On April 15th, at Weston, the parson at Easter received his customary 2s., at the hands of Terry, who also gave 6s. to a man for bringing a salmon out of Warwickshire (*sic.*). Other items during this Eastertide month were for oranges, 8d.; a sugar loaf presented to my lady, 6s.; to the cook's with[1] at Henwick,—where he had lately paid another visit— 2s. 6d.; 7 pairs of gloves, one pair being of hind-skin, 11s. 6d.; and a gift of 10s. to John Scott, the coachman, when he drove Francis from Moor Hall to Weston.

And now at last Spring was in the air, and there could be no more dalliance. So on April 27th Smyth records that Francis began his journey to London, and then turning over to a fresh page he heads it: "An account of my Master's and my Lady his mother's expenses in their journey to London occasioned upon my Master's marriage . . . .". Thus a new and great phase had begun.

[1] See p. 36.

CHAPTER IV

THE WEDDING AND THE HONEYMOON,
JUNE—SEPTEMBER, 1659

The accounts now of course become fuller and much more concentrated, and it is evident that Smyth was kept very busy until the wedding took place on June 7th, 1659. So on the last day of April, Lady Throckmorton and Francis drove up to London, once again in the old family coach, stopping on their way at the two accustomed stages. Her ladyship and her son drank ale on the road, and claret and sack at the two inns cost 2s. Oranges and lemons were bought during a halt at St Albans. Their other expenses amounted to £3 7s., and the next day two grooms were sent back to Weston with two of the four horses.

Soon after their arrival at their lodgings, Francis purchased 2 pairs of Spanish leather shoes, 9s., and took a hackney-coach to Paternoster Row, to see about a book which he wanted. Candles were also obtained, and 2 dozen of bottle ale, 7s., were ordered. Then he was trimmed at the barber's, 2s. 6d., where he also obtained the usual hair-powder and jessamy-butter; visited his tailors; and amongst other things paid for 12 ells of holland for 4 half-shirts, £4 4s.; bought a sword-blade and scabbard, 9s.; 2 glass inkhorns, 6d.; arranged for more lessons at the fencing and dancing-schools; and despatched some "sparagras", 2s. 6d., in a basket, 2d., to friends at Weston.

This was all good, but that wretched ague was once again at hand, and two days later fell upon him. So ale for my master in his ague at several times comes back cloudily into the accounts, but happily the attack does not seem to have been prolonged. Probably the purchase of a knitted waistcoat, 8s., a playbook, 1s., wine, and oranges and lemons, all had something to do with those fleeting days of brief inaction, for which Dr Woolfe's fees attending my master in his ague amounted to £2, the apothecary that administered

a clyster being paid 5s.   Francis also bought another
play-book, this being *Pastor Fido*[1]—thus noted by Smyth—
for which he gave 5s.

Then followed days of much coach-hire and the purchase
of a supply of ale—including 2 bottles of goat ale[2]—but
what was really of the first importance was that Anne
Monson had just reached London with her mother, and
attended by her maid, to whom Francis at once gave a
tactful 5s.   It was now all in the merry month of May, and
Francis having again been to his barber, this time buying
orange-butter[3] and hair-powder, took the bride-elect and
five of her relations to the Opera,[4] £1 10s., where he bought
her the play-book, 1s., of which unfortunately the title is
not given.   The next day there was a treat—thus Smyth
styles it—for all the party, spread out in one of the reserved
arbours at Marylebone Park, which cost Francis as much as
£2 19s. 6d.   He also hired two coaches for Hyde Park,
which were kept waiting there for some hours.   Two days
later they again went to Hyde Park, where the gatekeeper
was given 1s.   Other of Francis's personal expenses at this
time included more visits to the barber, a pair of pearl-silk
stockings, a pair of thread stockings, 2 pairs of socks,
£1 8s., and a new hilt for a sword, and the scouring of 2
swords, and for 2 new scabbards, 16s.   Mrs Monson and
Anne also, of course, had much shopping to do during this
brief period, throughout which Francis was usually in
attendance, and hackney-coaches were taken from place
to place.   On May 17th he gave another treat, this time at

[1] Giambattista Guarini's *Il Pastor Fido*, an Italian pastoral drama
first published in 1590 had been acted about 1605 at King's College,
in a Latin version, *Pastor Fidus*.   See *Cambridge History of English
Literature*, Vol. VI, 317.

[2] See p. 52, *n*. 2.

[3] An ointment perfumed with orange.

[4] Probably they went to hear Davenant's *The Siege of Rhodes*,
which was being performed at this time, and "became something of
a stock piece at Davenant's new theatre in Lincoln's Inn, which
Pepys actually calls 'The Opera', more than a dozen times in the
diary".   (E. Bloom, *Music in England*, p. 78. (1942).   "*The
Siege of Rhodes* is rightly claimed as the first English opera".
(A. Lowenberg, *Annals of Opera*, 1591–1940.   Pp. 17–18.   (1943).

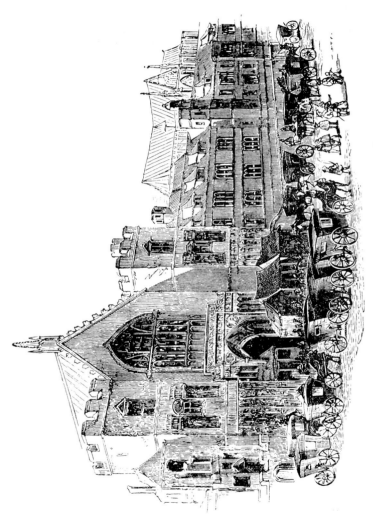

HACKNEY COACHES AT WESTMINSTER, 1637

Mulberry Garden[1] for Mrs Charles Carington.; made a gift of 2s. 6d. to a man who delivered a cabinet, being one of his presents to Anne; and called on Major Throckmorton, his best man, to discuss the arrangements for the wedding. On the 20th there was a third and more subdued treat for a party of six at Mulberry Garden, on which day 3 dozen of bottle ale cost 10s.—not this time as a part of the treat—and a visit was paid to the dancing-school, where the woman that swept the floor was given 1s.

Certainly Francis was paying particular attention to his personal appearance at this time, for he was soon again at his barber's to be trimmed—which included shaving—where he also bought more hair-powder and another pair of curling-irons. In addition to additional fencing-lessons he also arranged with the dancing-master for double teaching for one month, perhaps with a desire to satisfy Anne, who may have been a little exacting in the matter of his steps. Early in June he took her again to Mulberry Garden, accompanied by their friend, Mrs Gery, of Bushmead Priory.

The great event was now close at hand, and Mrs Stock-dall, their good landlady, who supplied all the diet for the Throckmortons—the party now consisting of "12 persons above and 5 below"[2]—was having a busy time. It is small wonder, therefore, that the betrothed were glad to get away from the lodgings of their respective mothers, and to seek peaceful and umbrageous paths, first at Hyde Park, then at Mulberry Garden, and later at Chelsea Park, where they

---

[1] Buckingham Palace now stands upon the site of Mulberry Garden, so called from the fact that James I had planted a mulberry garden there in 1609, at which time he had silk worms and the silk industry in mind. The Garden is mentioned in several 17th Century dramas, and it is interesting to note that certain authorities say that Cromwell had caused it to be closed—actually it was Spring Garden which he closed—some years before this time. Evelyn had been there on April 10th, 1654. He says: "My Lady Gerrard treated us at Mulberry Garden, now the only place of refreshment about the town for persons of the best quality to be exceedingly cheated at . . ." Pepys, in May, 1668, found Mulberry Garden "a very silly place, worse than Spring Garden, and but very little company, only a wilderness here, that is somewhat pretty". Referring to much later days, see W. M. Thackeray's description of a visit to Vauxhall Garden not long before the year 1815, *Vanity Fair*, Chapter VI.

[2] Perhaps above and below the salt.

went several times, and drank cider, ate cherries, and gave single money to those who begged of them.

Angier, the Cambridge tailor, had sent off the great trunk full of clothes by the carrier, to London, strongly corded, and protected with mats, and had some more pairs of silk stockings dyed for Francis.   On the preceding day he bought a wedding Indian gown—presumably a night-gown of fine Indian silk—for which he paid £4, in addition to £1 10s. for a cushion cloth[1] suitable to the gown, and 8s. for a pair of slippers.   He also bought an expensive new hat, £2, and the tailor—not the tailor's boy on this great occasion—that brought back his wedding suits,[2] had a gift of 10s.   There was then also a linen-box perfumed and lined—another little gift for the bride—bought on that wedding eve, and Francis was again trimmed by his barber, now named as being Prickett, who also sold him a pound of amber,[3] 5s. and several combs, 6s. 6d.

The day of the wedding, as already noted, was June 7th, but Smyth has naturally little to detail about it on his side. My lady's wedding-ring had been chosen, a modest £1 12s. 6d., and the bridegroom must of course be well supplied with ready-money, so Smyth handed him six gold guineas,[4] and on the wedding-day £3 10s., in silver, at which time a Mr Singleton was paid £3, possibly for the marriage licence.[5] The only other items were for hackney-coach hire; 2 dozen of bottle ale; and 4 bottles of sack and Rhenish wine on the

[1] Presumably, in this instance, a nightgown case, although it usually denominated a cushion cover.   See also p. 61.

[2] See p. 64.

[3] Amber gris or amber grease, used by perfumers and hairdressers as a scent.

[4] It is generally understood that the term 'guinea' did not take its rise until the Royal Mint was authorized to coin guineas—made of gold from Guinea—in 1663, but Smyth definitely uses it in this item, in June 7th, 1659.

[5] Even at this particular period, there was doubtless a religious as well as a civil ceremony.   In the previous century, on July 3rd, 1571, a license with special privileges had been issued to members of two Roman Catholic families, Francis Throckmorton—Francis's unfortunate ancestor—son and heir of Sir John Throckmorton, to marry with Anne Sutton alias Dudley, one of the heirs of Edward Sutton (Lord Dudley), without the proclamation of banns, in any church, chapel, or oratory in the diocese of Worcester, by any fit priest.

wedding night, a very limited expense. There is no direct evidence as to who were the guests at the wedding, with the exception of Francis's mother, who now became the dowager, and married Lewis Mordaunt not long afterwards.

On the day after the wedding, two coaches were hired to take a little party to Marrowbone [Marylebone] Park,[1] where there must, of course, be very special music, to which Francis gave £1. There were also more great flourishes of trumpets for these joyous visitors, Francis giving 10s. to 2 sets of trumpets, and £1 10s. to several companies of trumpets and music. Altogether, at least on their arrival, it must have been somewhat of a wedding pandemonium, to which was added the pleading of the poor, who got 4s. amongst them. However, all this could not have taken up very much time on that long and presumably glorious day in June, during which the two coachmen and their coaches were kept waiting for 10 hours.

Two days later Francis went back to his chambers somewhere near the Old Bailey, where he drank ale, and packed his trunks—this time keeping the coachman waiting for four hours. He then returned with them to Mrs Rake's house, where he and his bride now had their lodgings, with four of the Weston servants, including Parsons, to attend on them.

The next ten pages of the accounts are mainly concerned with details of bills more or less associated with the wedding, the first being Mrs Constable's bill for my master's wedding linen. This consisted of 1⅜ yards of lace at £3 per yard, £4 2s. 6d., for cloth, and for making the wedding band or ruff, 3s., 1⅜ yards of lace at 22s. a yard, £1 10s. 3d., 1⅜ yards of lace at 30s. a yard, £2 1s. 3d., 3 ells of holland for his wedding shirts, £4 8s., making 2 shirts and bands to them, 10s., 1 doz. of lane[2] bands, £1 16s., 6 pocket-handkerchiefs, £1 7s., a laced night cap, 16s., 2 combing cloths and 2 cushion cloths, £1 11s., lace for the shirt bands, 5s., and 8 garnish[3] of buttons for the handkerchiefs[4] and the cushion

[1] Well known to Pepys. It was closed in 1778, and now forms a part of Regent's Park.
[2] Lawn.
[3] Sets.
[4] See p. 47.

cloths, and 2 pairs of band-strings, £2 13s. For making 9 shirts and 7 half-shirts, £1 12s. was also paid.

The old family-coach was still in some London stables, but not used, and the two horses also retained there cost Francis 8d. a night for 48 nights. Whilst the coach had been in London it—and even the harness too—had had to be mended, £2 7s. 6d., and it is quite evident that it simply would not do for this youthful Lady Throckmorton. They really must have a new one, and so the old one was now sold for a mere song, after all its travels and adventures. Poor old coach, what stories it could have told!

And what of the new one? There is no evidence as to who built it, for he is simply called the coach-maker, and was paid £28 for making it. With it were supplied 9¾ yards of Spanish cloth, with which it was lined, £6 12s. 6d., 5 yards of baize to line the coach-boots, 10s., 5½ yards of serge for curtains, £1, 25½ yards of fringe, £3 5s., 8½ yards of baize to line the rolling-doors[1] and cover the seats, 17s., and 6 doz. curtain-rings, 4s. The coachmaker was also paid for 2 sets of harness for 4 horses, £10; the young men that made the harness were given 2s. between them; and 2s. 6d. was the cost of the hamper to carry down the harness to Weston. Then there must of course be a canvas covering, £1 15s., for this new coach, when at home in its coach-house. This was the final item, at least as concerning the actual coach, of which the total cost was £51 18s.[2] However the matter did not end there, for at Weston it was found that a new coach-house had to be built too, either because the old coach-house was too small, or because the new coach was too smart for the old quarters of its modest and shabby predecessor. So, as time goes on, various relevant building expenses, into which it is not necessary to go, are detailed in the accounts, and when finished the coach-house was thatched, strong doors being provided to protect it from intruders, and paths made which led up to it.

[1] Somewhat of an innovation.

[2] For comparison, in 1634 a new coach for the Provost of King's College, Cambridge, cost £42 15s. 4d.; and in 1668, Pepys paid £53 for his coach, the coachmaker "to stand to the courtesy of what more I should give him upon the finishing of the coach. . ." For a later (1777) private coach and its accessories (£88), see Notes and Queries, October 18th, 1941, p. 213.

The whole of the honeymoon was spent in London, during which time there was again much shopping to do, often with a rebeautified Weston House in mind. On one of these occasions Francis and Anne went off into the city, to Mr Smith's the goldsmith, with whom they spent £29 5s., roughly made up as follows:—A silver salver at 5s. 10d. per oz., £10 5s., a silver cup and cover at 6s. per oz., £7 14s. 4d., a silver matted[1] cup and cover with ears, £4 15s. 6d., a silver maudlen[2] cup and cover, £6 6s. 3d. All these pieces were at the same time engraved with the arms[3] of the Throckmortons, at 12d. per coat.

Then there was a visit to Mr Hemes of the New Exchange, at whose shop that same June day the young couple paid £6 17s. for certain little gifts which had been made to some of the chief wedding guests shortly before the ceremony. Thus there was an embroidered pair of gloves for the best man, Major Throckmorton, who was also given a pair of white gloves, £1 11s. 8d. As for the other men, Sir Thomas Smyth, Edward Guldeford and George Gery each had a pair of cordevan[4] and a pair of white gloves, altogether 14s.; and Thomas and Harry Salwey each had a pair of fringe gloves at 8s. per pair, and a pair of white gloves at 1s. 8d. per pair. Thus all the men wore white gloves for the ceremony, the other gloves being for use immediately afterwards. Lady Throckmorton—the dowager—had a present of no less than 12 pairs of gauntlet gloves, 16s., and a ribbon muff, 17s.; Mrs Guldeford, a lace scarf, £1 10s.; and there were 2 hoods[5] for Mrs Gery, 9s.

A week or two later Francis and Anne went to the pewterer's, whose name is not given, of whom they ordered 10 dishes weighing 14½ lbs. each at 14d. per lb., 2 chargers,

[1] Of roughened or figured groundwork.
[2] A covered cup. One of the emblems of St Mary Magdalene, perhaps representative of the "alabaster box", e.g. on the statue of the saint in Henry the Seventh's Chapel, Westminster Abbey.
[3] They are: Gules on a chevron argent three bars gemel sable, crest, an elephant's head. Motto *Virtus sola nobilitas*.
[4] Spanish leather from Cordova. Cordova leather, according to some authorities, was also manufactured, mostly in England, from goat-skin.
[5] At this period women mostly went bareheaded, but often wore hoods in rough weather.

40 lbs. each at 14d. per lb., and a pasty plate, 13¼ lbs. at
15d. per lb.   The engraving of 26 coats of arms on the dishes
cost 17s. 4d., and for engraving 6 brass candle-sticks with
double coats[1]—the candlesticks seem to have been a
wedding-present made to them by one of their friends—the
pewterer was paid 12s., and there was 5s. for a hamper,
cord and porterage, when eventually all these things were
sent down to Weston.

On July 2nd, Airie, a London tailor, was paid the large
sum of £170, for clothes for Francis and three of his servants,
which had been supplied between November 10th, 1658, and
his wedding-day.   In November he had had a black suit
and a cloak, £11 5s. 9d., and 2 pairs of drawers lined with
cotton, 6s. 6d.   At the end of the following April, £18 8s. 3d.
was paid for cloth linings, and making up his greenish coloured
cloth suit and coat, lined with tabby.   A fortnight later he
had a mingled colour stuff suit and coat lined with tabby,
and laced[2] with buttons, £16 18s. 5d.; and on June 6th—
the day before his marriage—his wedding-suit had arrived,
very expensive, of feathered tabby, and coat laced with
silver lace, and trimmed with silver ribbons, £41 8s. 8d.
Later on there is an item of £3 7s. paid for new trimming of
this suit, the silver ribbons being taken off at the wedding,
which seems to suggest that the guests had claimed them as
souvenirs.   There certainly were 17th Century instances
in which bridegrooms were thus similarly despoiled of their
glories, but in this case it is far more probable that Francis
desired this significant suit to be made less so, for normal
wear.

Another expensive suit—the honeymoon suit—was of
light colour cloth . . . and coat lined with tabby, laced and
tufted,[3] £37 11s. 10d., and there was also a gray camlet[4] coat
lined with serge, £3 10s.   Then there was a drugget[5] riding

[1] Of Throckmorton and of Monson, or perhaps Throckmorton
impaling Monson.
[2] Adorned.
[3] With tassels.
[4] Of mixed materials, see S. W. Beck's *The Draper's Dictionary*,
(1886), pp. 48–50. Pepys, on June 1st, 1664, "put on my new
camelott suit, the best I ever wore in my life, the suit costing me
above £24".
[5] A sort of woollen stuff.

suit and coat lined with tabby, and 2 pairs of holland stockings,[1] £12 10s. 10d.; and the ribbons of the greenish suit, already mentioned, were smoothed and new set, 3s. 8d. Finally, one of the servants had a black serge suit, £2 16s. 4d., which was very modest in comparison with the coachman's and footman's suits and coats laced, and for stockings and a feather[2] for the footman, £21 18s. 2d. in all.

A few weeks later Anne's maid purchased many things for her, the items filling a page of the accounts, and amounting to £5 11s. 8d. They included a looking-glass, almond-powder,[3] jessamy-butter, patches, a hood and a white fan, white gloves (14 pairs), many yards of ribbon of different sorts and colours, several pairs of thread stockings, some ounces of silk and thread, much tape, some starch and blue, and needles and pins. About this time a mask[4] or vizard, 2s. 6d., was also bought. Later on there was another account defrayed by Smyth which included 3 lbs. of damask powder and the making of the sweet bags,[5] 14s., a basket quilted with perfumes,[6] £1 3s. 6d., and a cushion box, 7s. 6d.

During these summer days there were also many smaller purchases, amongst them being almonds, lemons, raspberries, and gooseberries. Then Anne's diamond ring—perhaps an heirloom—needed a new setting, 15s., and her watch was mended, at which time she bought a case for it, £1 2s.

Towards the end of June a great trunk with drawers, 16s., had been bought, which was now filled and despatched to Weston by the carrier's waggon, together with a port mantue—thus Smyth—10s., and much other baggage, all done up in packing-cloth and well-corded. It chiefly consisted of purchases which Francis and Anne had made

[1] To wear beneath other stockings.

[2] In fine feather for the wedding. Sir John Reresby, in his *Memoirs*, under May 10th, 1658, writes: "Walking one day in the street with my valet de chambre, who did wear a feather in his hat . . ."

[3] Of a delicate pink colour, for the gloves.

[4] Of velvet or silk, and probably worn, as ladies were accustomed to do at that period, when Anne went in the evening with Francis to Mulberry Garden, or some such resort. In September, 1667, Pepys and his wife visited Bartholomew Fair, she wearing a vizard. These were linen masks at 10d., but such were not for Anne or Mrs Pepys.

[5] Scented sachets.

[6] Quilted and scented.

for the old mansion, which had naturally fallen into a rather neglected condition during those recent difficult years.   They included a bed and its furniture, with 7 chairs and stools, £23, 2 rugs and 2 pairs of blankets and a holland quilt, £6 9s., 2 small rugs, 18s., an oval table, £3 5s., 5 pieces of hangings, £30, and 6 Turkey-work chairs, £4 16s. The total weight of the load was 11 cwt. 3 qrs. 20 lbs., and the cost of transit, £3 3s. 8d.

To Weston they also sent 12 artichokes,[1] 4s. 6d., together with oranges and lemons, 2s. 8d., all in a basket, as a little present for the dowager.

Shortly before leaving London, Francis went to Mr Harvey the Vintner's where he bought 9 gallons of claret, £1 10s., together with 3 dozen glass bottles and corks, 18s., and a hamper.   Harvey's sign, as is noted by Smyth, was the St John's Head, where Francis also spent 1s. 7d. on this occasion of choosing his wine.   During this time he had had an earlier deal with Harvey, when he bought 12½ gallons of canary and 12¾ gallons of claret, £7 2s. 6d., all afterwards sent off to Weston; and about the same time a pottle[2] and a half of claret, 1s. 10½d., sent to my lady's lodgings, was a sample for her approval before Francis confirmed his choice.

This was on June 23rd, and on the previous day Brewer, the oilman, had been paid for 2 quarts of olive oil, 4s. 6d., olives and capers, 4s. 4d., 6 neats' tongues, 16s. 6d., anchovies,[3] 1s. 8d., and 2 barrels of pickled oysters.   About the same time Smyth took a coach to carry Mrs Tresham's[4] £200 in specie to some unspecified destination; and Francis and Anne went to their favourite Mulberry Garden once more, where they kept the coachman waiting for five hours.

---

[1] 1655. Moffett and Benn, *Health's Improvement*, p. 312: "Artichokes grow sometimes only in the Isle of Sicily, and since my remembrance they were so dainty in England, that usually they were sold for Crowns a-piece".   (*O.E.D.*).

[2] Two quarts.

[3] Pepys, on one occasion, gave some visitors "anchovies and ham of bacon", and later on, "a pretty dish of anchovies and sweetmeats".

[4] A connexion by marriage with the Treshams of Lyvden, near Oundle, co. Northampton. Francis Tresham, the betrayer of the Gunpowder Plot, was the eldest son of Sir Thomas Tresham, by his wife Muriel, daughter of Sir Robert Throckmorton, of Coughton Court, grandfather of Francis.   He was decapitated, and his head set over the gates at Northampton.

A few days later some syrup of mulberries and Jew's ears,[1] 1s. 2d., had been bought, and also a red plaster, 2s., for Francis had been unwell again.

It was now early in July, and these honeymoon days must come to their close. Francis and Anne had begun to know London fairly well by now, that crowded little metropolis— with its many filthy streets and lanes—which only a few years later was to be decimated by the Great Plague, and almost overwhelmed by the Great Fire, of both of which calamities Pepys saw so much and has so much to say.

On the day before they returned to Weston, they decided to go and see how the men were getting on with the new coach. So they hired a hackney-coach, 2s.—when my lady went to see her new coach—and there was Smyth still always at hand, to produce and to account for even this trivial payment. It would seem, however, that Francis had made up his mind that this system, which was all very well when he was younger, was now undignified and must soon end, as happened not long afterwards.

When they reached the coachmaker's it at once became evident that the work had not proceeded as quickly as had been expected. Indeed it was a question if the coach would be ready to take them in great array to Weston. This was unfortunate, but—at my lady's desire—in any case it must also be garnished with silk curtains, and the coachmaker's men were to have 2s. 6d. amongst them, to which Francis agreed, and 4 bottles of beer, 8d., were also given to them to mark the occasion.

So there was nothing for it but to hire a coach, and to leave a deposit of 10s. with the coachman as an earnest. Thus, in this more modest state, they started off for Weston on July 15th, Anne buying a coif, 4s. 6d. to wear on the dusty way thither, and also cherries, which they consumed—and the coachman had beer—whilst making a brief stop at Highgate. The journey—during which the coach broke down, 4s. 6d. being paid for mending it—was made in the

---

[1] The popular name of a fungus known botanically as Hirucola auricula-judae, so called from its shape, which somewhat resembled a human ear. It was formerly prescribed as a remedy for dropsy. (*Encycl. Brit.*).

customary two stages, their total expenses being £2 16s. 4d., exclusive of the coach, for which they were charged £3 7s. 6d.

Of course the church bells of Olney were joyously rung, and those of Weston gave them a familiar welcome, £1 10s. being distributed by Francis amongst the two bands of ringers. The coachman was only given 2s. 6d. as a gratuity, so it may be that he had arranged to get other passengers for his return journey to London, as had been done on a previous occasion.

Another gift was of 5s. to the maids that strewed the street with flowers[1] at my lady's first coming. It is thus that the gallant Smyth graphically describes the pleasant little scene as the happy pair drove into the little village, on the Olney end of which the Throckmorton mansion was situated. However, the maids—or at least the onlookers—must have been not a little disappointed when the hired coach came into view instead of the new family-coach of which everyone had already heard, for that new coach-house had also been hurriedly built for its reception.

Francis, now once more at Weston, resumed his accustomed country-life, and went hunting the fox in Sawsy Forest,[2] at which time he gave money to the keepers. Hitherto he had shown little inclination for this form of sport, and his horsemanship can never have been very impressive, except so far as it concerned himself and his various falls. It is not surprising, therefore, to find that on one of these occasions a man that broke the hedge to let my master forth, and for making it up again, was rewarded with 6d. At this time the Weston stables—near which a well had been recently sunk—were being repaired, and money was paid for sawing of sleepers[3] for the stables.

Francis had had horses sent up for their use in the park and elsewhere during their stay. There is no record of their baiting, indeed all expenses of this type slowly fade out of the accounts, which are now more or less confined to household affairs at Weston, including payments for diet for the

---

[1] The only mention of any flowers throughout the accounts.

[2] Salcey Forest, a few miles from Weston, and just over the Northamptonshire border.

[3] A somewhat early use of the word.

household generally, which usually included at least seven servants. All the laundry-work was undertaken by a woman, who came in from the village several days every week, sometimes accompanied by another woman "that did char".

There was now some playing at labet, whatever that may have been, and more shovel-board—they had no billiard-table at Weston—and about this time Smyth delivered to my lady at cards at twice, £1 0s. 6d. and more to her lap—more for her pocket—his usual way of expressing it, £1. Francis also took her to see John Digby's coal-pits, now untraceable. The distance cannot have been far from Weston—possibly at Hanslope, where the Digbys had other property—and Anne may not have found it a very thrilling expedition.

Mrs Monson had now also arrived at Weston, to pay a first and short visit, during which she temporarily lent her son-in-law 4 pieces of gold, but there is no evidence that the dowager was there too. On July 25th Francis went to Northampton Fair, where he met and dined with Charles Carington, John Mordaunt, Dr Hernshaw, and Richard Kempson. This visit to Northampton was undertaken for the purpose of buying a pair of coach-horses, £39, to make up the four for the new coach—which had now been delivered at Weston—an additional item of 2 aprons to preserve the coach-horses from gelding, costing 2s. 10d.

A little later Francis and Anne paid a visit to the Fortescues at Salden, and to the Lowes at Clifton Reynes, where Anne played at her favourite labet, and Francis played at shovel-board and tables[1] with James Lowe, to whom he lost £1 10s., and also 5s. at a horse-match, to which they all went. The next day the Lowes' cook was rewarded with 2s. 6d., and Francis and Anne returned to Weston, but it was not long before he was back again at Clifton Reynes, where Lowe ran a race and Francis lost £2 10s. in bets on it. About this time Lowe had, for the time being, far too deep a finger in his friend's not very fruitful pie, and particularly as concerning his horses at Weston.

On August 12th Smyth went up to London, his expenses

[1] Backgammon.

and his pass[1] costing 16s. 6d. this being the only reference
to a recusant's pass throughout all these accounts. He had
gone there to make arrangements for the young couple who,
however, only remained in London for a very short time.
Whilst there, Smyth was called upon to produce 18s. 6d.
for Francis for a loss at cards; he also delivered to my lady
in gold and silver, £1 15s., and soon afterwards a further
13s. 6d., for her to play at labet. It was at this time, too,
that Anne's great cabinet, an expensive piece costing £52,
was delivered at Weston; and Francis presented some
friends there—Mr and Mrs Jefferies and their son and
daughter—with gloves, together with two hoods for the
ladies, £3.

On September 13th one of the Weston keepers brought a
haunch of venison upon my master's birthday, and a side
of venison came from another source. From this venison
a number of festal pasties were made, one being sent to
Mrs Gery, and Anne—who a little later on received a cake
sent to her from Budbrooke—celebrated her husband's
19th anniversary by playing more cards than usual, interspersed sometimes with dice, now at higher stakes. She
also went down to Olney to buy some of its already celebrated bone-lace, together with ribbons and many pairs of
gloves.

They and some friends all drove and rode over to Bunsty
Oak, near Gayhurst and Newport Pagnell, for this birthday
occasion, which could not have been very exciting, for it
only cost them 1s. 6d., and they took with them some white
wine[2] and almonds, for which Anne had a liking. The butler
added to the dignity of this rustic occasion, and there was
also a footboy in attendance. The Lowes, later in the

---

[1] *Cf.* Joan Parkes, *Travel in England in the 17th Century*,
(1925), p. 37. Amongst the documents preserved at Coughton
Court in 1672, and doubtless still there, are "Licences to Recusants,
permitting them to travel beyond 5 miles from their usual place of
residence, granted to members of the Throckmorton family from
1618 to 1639, with a few dated in 1645–1671. A folio volume"
(Hist. MSS. Comm., 3rd Report, p. 257).

[2] This reference to white wine is a reminder of two additional items
with which it is concerned about this time:—"For white wine for
caudles", 1s., and "For lemons, white wine, and sugar for caudles",
1s. 3d.

month, again invited them to dine at their house, at which
time Francis gave 5s. to the music, which after all would
not seem to have been his affair, but such may have been
customary at that period. At least it was a custom with
him, as these accounts testify on a variety of occasions.
Shortly afterwards they stayed with the Tyringhams,
when Francis and Anne again played at labet, losing
between them as much as £3 18s.

Earlier in October Francis had a day's hunting with my
Lord Bruce,[1] whom he entertained at Olney. Then, at last,
Mrs Monson, the mother-in-law, left Weston, and the
young people at once betook themselves to Northampton,
going there in the new coach. The next day Anne returned
therein to Weston, and Francis—having arranged for horses
for himself and his man—rode on to Weldon, and so to
Market Harborough, in the Leicester district, to the horse-
fair there, paying a penny toll[2] at Billing Bridge, on the road
between Northampton and Wellingborough. At the inn
at Market Harborough he entertained lavishly, for him,
spending £4 10s. 6d. whilst there for that one night. At the
fair he bought a bay gelding, £4 15s.

Hunting—when my master did hunt the fox—was now
very much in vogue over a wide district, so Francis had a
huntsman[3] installed at Weston, doubtless because he already
knew that Colonel Throckmorton intended to present him
with a pack of dogs. The pack duly arrived on November
7th, the kennels having been prepared for them. A new
furnace to boil the dogs' meat, £1 8s. 6d., was set up in the
stableyard, and from time to time the carcase of a poor
dog-horse—only fit for the dogs—was bought and cut up
to provide that meat. On occasions the dogs were also given
mutton, oatmeal, and graves[4]; and the huntsman was
furnished with a great knife with which to cut up the dogs'

---

[1] At that time living at Ampthill, Bedfordshire.

[2] The only toll noted in the accounts.

[3] Another servant, Harry Boult, who makes a number of appear-
ances in the accounts, "lay out one night hunting of the fox", early
in February, 1659–60.

[4] Graves. The refuse of meat, skin, and fat from the process of
tallow-making, pressed into large blocks, and sold as food for dogs.
(O.E.D.).

meat. Various neighbouring friends had also sent several couples of hounds to join the pack—with which they were all going to hunt—and others were also brought out of Warwickshire.

In the afternoon of the day on which the Colonel's pack arrived at Weston, Francis and Anne went out to dine at Sir Harry Elverton's house, not very far away, and on their return—after a good deal of card playing—got so benighted, or befogged, that they had to pay 2s. to the man that guided the coach in the night along the road to Weston. Jack Parsons was the coachman, and later on Anne gave instructions that he should have 2s. 6d. extra to his small wage, in grateful token of when he drove the coach to Sir Harry Elverton's house and back, under such difficult conditions. At this time she then ordered more wood for her chamber, the weather being very cold, and also paid for 2 standard candlesticks.[1] About All Saints' Day (November 1st)—one of the very few references to a Church Festival—Smyth paid for the hire of a horse for a Mr Scull, to go to Oxford upon my master's and Mrs Monson's business, concerning which some letters for Oxford had already been entrusted to the carrier as he passed through Weston.

More hunting, and then on November 24th money was given to the men that were hunting the fox, and dug him out, and to Sir Anthony Chester's huntsman; and later to an earthstopper at Dungy; and so on. However, vaulting ambition o'erleaped itself. Francis, who had just bought a new pair of riding-boots and spurs, £1 3s., again fell from his horse, and his good friend, Dr Medford, was called in, his fee being £1.

At Christmas the mummers were twice at Weston Hall, where there was much music, and £1 was distributed amongst the poor of the village, and others to whom at the New Year small gifts were also made. Francis had now quite recovered from his fall, and on January 23rd, 1659-60, he went to Sir Anthony Chester's house[2] where my master and Colonel Throckmorton, with Mr Thwaites, dined when they hunted the fox.

---

[1] These may have been provided for the little chapel which had long been in the house.

[2] At Chicheley, near Newport Pagnell.

On St Valentine's Day, upon which there was again music, Francis, as in his Cambridge days, again gave his valentines—his presents—but this time they only cost a few shillings, and apparently Anne did not receive one. A few days later there is an item of £4 paid to Prickett, the London barber, for 2 periwigs which Francis gave as a present to Ambrose Throckmorton.

About the middle of March, Francis and Anne drove to Newport Pagnell, when my master brought my lady towards London, and she was there, with her mother, when the Protectorate came to its feeble close, and March 29th, 1660, dawned triumphantly for the Restoration, and for them all —fervent Royalists as they were. There is, however, no reference to this historic event, for Smyth's connexion with these accounts had—unfortunately for us—come to its end, a few days before, on Lady Day. Thus he writes the following statement, duly signed by Francis:—

"All the accounts of James Smyth from the first time he came unto my service until this present 25th day of March, 1660, have been perused, made even, and allowed by me, Francis Throckmorton, and also I have received forty-three shillings and tenpence of him, to level these accounts. In witness that I do allow of all his said accounts, and all the premises, I have hereunto put my hand the day and year above written. Francis Throckmorton".

F

Thus this faithful stewardship had ended, and Francis had now really become his own master. He had only first signed Smyth's accounts on October 4th, 1659, four months after his marriage, and he continued to do so from time to time until their close. Smyth always wrote the formal certificate of examination, beneath which Francis made his good, flowing signature,[1] instances of which still sparkle with the sand which sprinkled over them from the sandbox on his standish. Even now he was only in his twentieth year, and life had so far been comparatively easy for him, under very difficult circumstances. His mother, who was now nearing her fiftieth year, had—as already noted—married Lewis Mordaunt, and they were living at Mordaunt's ancestral home at Walton. Probably this was soon after Francis and Anne had married, for following their arrival at Weston in July, 1659, no further reference is made to his mother, and the young people reigned supreme there, and at Moor Hall, where they also spent a good deal of time in those first years together.

[1] It would seem that nothing else in his handwriting is now known to exist.

Chapter V

IN LATER YEARS

At first, research—so far as it has been possible in these days—did not prove at all productive concerning the later years of Francis's comparatively short life, and there seemed to be nothing to chronicle for that period, apart from the information which is supplied by three documents still in existence. Two of them are now affixed to blank pages in Smyth's ledger, and are dated in the years 1663 and 1666 respectively. They read as follows:—

(i) To the Right Hon. the Lord Treasurer of England, to the Baron of the Exchequer, and to the Commissioners for the County of Surrey, and all others whom it may concern:

'These are to certify that Sir Francis Throckmorton of Moor Hall within the Constabulary of Wixford in the county of Warwick, Baronet, being resident with his family at Moor Hall aforesaid within the said Constabulary is there taxed and assessed at £26 6s. 8d. in lands for his whole estate within the County of Warwick and for all other his estate and estates within the County of Surrey for and towards the payment of the two first of the four entire subsidies, payable before the first of November, 1663, according to the late Act of Parliament granted to his Majesty in the 15th year of his reign for the raising of the said four subsidies.

'In witness whereof we as Commissioners amongst others nominated in the said Act of Parliament for the said County of Warwick have hereunto set our hands and seals the third day of October, Anno Domini, 1663.

'[Signed and sealed]   Charles Lee[1]
                        W. Somervile[2]
                        Tho. Rawlins.[3]'...... ....

[1] Of Billesley Hall, some three miles from Stratford-on-Avon. In the Domestic State Papers (1683, p. 191) there is an interesting letter which he wrote, on April 19th, 1683, to his friend and neighbour, the Earl of Conway, at Ragley Hall, near Alcester. See also *Visitation of Warwickshire*, (1682–3). (Harl. Soc., Vol. 62. pp. 70–1).
[2] Of Edstone, in the parish of Wootton Wawen.
[3] Of Pophills, in the parish of Salford Priors.

(ii) 'A Commission to Sir Francis Throckmorton to raise a Troop of Horse, 1666'.

'Kidderminster, July 16th, 1666.

'Gentlemen,

'Upon seeing a letter or rather a command from you to Sir Francis Throckmorton to desist listing any volunteers for the King's service in case of an invasion, I think fit to acquaint you that I did authorize (by the advice of the Deputy Lieutenants of this County) Sir Francis Throckmorton to make preparation for the having a troop of Volunteer Horse to serve under me upon forty-eight hours warning as Lieutenant of this County in case any invasion[1] should be made upon His Majesty's Kingdom of England. I am, Gentlemen,

'Your very humble servant

Windsor'.

'Vera copia
　Charles Lee'.

On January 13th, 1665–66, a few months before, as recorded in the contemporary minutes of the Corporation of Evesham, "Sir Francis Throgmorton and Thomas, Lord Windsor[1] (Lord Lieutenant of Worcestershire), were elected Freemen of the Borough of Evesham".

Written on the back of this letter, and by the same hand—which, with the exception of the signature, is not that of Francis—is the following:—

'Sir,　　　　　　　　　　　　　　　　　　[No date].

'I having an estate in Worcestershire, am upon that account empowered by the Lord Windsor to raise a troop of horse for His Majesty's service in case of an invasion, to be ready in 48 hours. In order to that commission I did intend to list,[2] and declared in several places I had such a commission, but never intended to list any of the militia of this or any other county, but did believe I might have raised a troop in this or any other county

---

[1] Created Earl of Plymouth in 1682, see also p. 38.
[2] List. To have one's name entered upon the list of a military body (*N.E.D.*).

upon so just a cause,[1] only it was my misfortune that Sir Charles Lee dined not at home [at Billesley] on Monday last. If he had, I had waited on him and acquainted him with it. For the future I shall forbear to list any in this county, and remain, Sir

Your faithful servant

[Signed] Francis Throckmorton'.

(iii) In 1673 Francis received the appointment of Cupbearer in Ordinary to Queen Catherine of Braganza, the unhappy and haughty wife of Charles II. This appointment was probably pleasing to him, although under all the circumstances it did not mean very much. Originally the Cupbearer's duty had been to serve the Queen with drink on bended knee, having first tasted the liquor in the cup. At that time the salary was one hundred marks (£33 6s. 8d.) per annum. This certificate of Francis's appointment read thus:

'Henry, Lord Cornbury,[2] Lord Chamberlain to the Queen's Majesty—

'These are to certify that Sir Francis Throckmorton is Cupbearer in Ordinary to Her Majesty, by virtue of which place he is to enjoy all rights and privileges thereunto belonging, in as full and ample manner to all intents and purposes as any other person or persons in the like place have formerly enjoined the same.

'Given under my hand and seal this sixteenth day of June in the twenty-fifth year of His Majesty's reign Annoque Domini 1673.

H. Cornbury[1]'.

[Endorsed:] 'Sir Francis Throckmorton's Patent that he is the Queen's Cupbearer in Ordinary, June 16th, 1673'.

---

[1] Apparently because, under the pressing circumstances, the troop had in the meantime been raised by someone else.

[2] Henry Hyde, second Earl of Clarendon. He was Private Secretary to Queen Catherine in 1662, and Chamberlain in 1665. An intimate friend of John Evelyn.

CHAPTER VI

DEATH AND FUNERAL
NOVEMBER—DECEMBER, 1680

These accounts have consistently shown that Francis was never very physically strong, and therefore it is not surprising that he died soon after he had only completed his fortieth year. His death took place "at London",—simply that—on November 7th, 1680, as aforesaid, and as is evidenced not only on his imposing memorial now to be seen at the east end of the south aisle in Weston Church, but also in the fully-detailed "Disbursements upon Sir Francis Throckmorton's Funeral", which still exist. They do not, of course, form a section of Smyth's ledger, but are fully detailed on several pages, detached many years ago from a second and taller ledger which was doubtless unfortunately destroyed at the time that these pages were removed. They are now to be found loose in Smyth's old ledger. Possibly the second ledger contained the accounts of Francis's expenditure during some of the later years of his life, his house-steward then being John Burbery,[1] who was responsible for the payment of all the funeral disbursements.

For many years it has been considered—and the reason why will shortly appear—that Francis was buried at Weston, but these disbursements definitely prove that such was not the case. The burial actually took place at Chiversfield (now Chisfield), near Stevenage, amid charming and typical Hertfordshire surroundings. At Chisfield,[2] hidden remotely away, there is still the pathetically ruined little church of St Etheldreda, almost buried beneath masses of ivy, not far distant from the manor-house—Chisfield Park[3]—in these days included in the parish of Graveley, a village

[1] He came of a Coughton family.

[2] Sir H. Chauncy, _Antiquities of Hertfordshire_, (1726), Vol. II, pp. 125–26; W. F. Andrews, _The Ruined Church of Chisfield, Stevenage_, Trans. East Hertfordshire Archaeological Soc., 1902; V.C.H., _Hertfordshire_, (1912), Vol. III, p. 90, with a contemporary illustration of the ruins of Chisfield Church.

[3] The present mansion, erected shortly after 1680, stands in an extensive and well-wooded park. It is now the (1944) seat of Mrs Charles Poyntz-Stewart.

MOOR HALL IN 1939

(Photo: F. C. Morgan, F.S.A.)

CHISFIELD PARK IN 1850

(From "The County Seats of England")

with an interesting church, situated more openly just off the Great North Road, between Stevenage and Baldock.

There is no direct evidence to show why Francis was not buried at Weston, or indeed at distant Coughton, whither his remains were removed at a later date. Chisfield, however, certainly possessed some family associations, for his relative, George Throckmorton, who died in 1696, had married Elizabeth,[1] daughter and co-heir of William Clarke, who owned Chisfield. They were living at Chisfield Park at the time of the funeral, in connexion with which, as will transpire, they took in several people as paying guests.

The funeral—in striking contrast to the unostentatious life which Francis had lived—was a pompous proceeding, throughout which it will be noted that there is no reference to his widow, Lady Anne, who did not die until 1728. This omission seemed significant, and recent research, as will be shown,[2] has doubtless proved the cause from which it arose, and which indeed may also account for the burial at Chisfield and not at Weston.

On the day following his death the body of Francis was embalmed, one Higgins being paid £20 for this cereclothing. Cloth for mourning, and baize with which to hang the rooms of the house in which he died cost £50, paid to Bankes, a woollen-draper; and Jasper Walker, who had been a witness to deceased's will and was also a woollen draper, was paid £30 6s. for men's mourning. Edward Barker was paid £6 18s. 6d. for mourning cloth, for young Sir Robert Throckmorton, the heir—who had succeeded as such on the death of his brother, Francis, at Bruges, September 10th, 1676, aged 16—and for Dawley, one of the executors; and West, a mercer, for crape and other necessaries for the funeral, was paid £34 14s. 6d.

Hamper, a milliner, for gloves, scarves, etc. served in at the funeral, was paid £11 8s.; Philip Pinckney, a goldsmith,

---

[1] See an interesting letter written to her, in 1689, by a former manservant, concerning the treatment of "Papist Soldiers" at Chester (Domestic State Papers, 1689–90, pp. 141–2). She had been baptized at Chisfield in February, 1646–7. The Chisfield baptisms and marriages are recorded in the Graveley parish registers, which begin in 1551.

[2] See Chapter VII.

for mourning rings distributed at the funeral, £17 12s. 6d.;
and one Valley, a wax chandler, for wax candles, torches,
and flambeaux, used at the funeral, supplies an item which,
also in conjunction with a later one, evidences that, both in
London and at Chisfield, a room[1] was converted into a
chapelle ardente, and that the burial took place at night—
as was then of course somewhat fashionable, particularly in
high society—hence the torches and the flambeaux. Next
comes the most expensive item in these disbursements,
being the payment of £60 to Mr Wallis, a herald-painter,
for banners, flags, escutcheons,[2] and other ensigns of honour,
the testator expressly appointing by his will to be buried
according to his degree and quality. The painting of all
these accessories necessarily took a little time, and the
actual funeral—the body having been already embalmed—
awaited their completion.

For making Misses Anne[3] and Mary[4] Throckmorton's
mourning gowns, Mr Caham was paid the comparatively
modest sum of £3 18s.: Mr Biddle, a tailor, supplied the
servants' mourning, costing £4 5s.; and Mr Browne, a
tailor, for making the testator's daughters and their servants'
manto gowns[5] of crape was paid £2; Mr Wakeman, a tailor,
for making a suit for Mr Tatham, one of the bearers of the
corpse, and finding some materials, £4 7s.; and Mr Barradell,
a tailor, for making the mourning suits and finding some
materials for Sir Robert Throckmorton, Mr Clarke,[6] his
tutor, and for another bearer, £7 5s.

[1] It must have looked very much like the room described by the
Hon. Roger North, when writing of the obsequies of Sir Dudley
North, who died in London some eleven years later. He wrote:
". . . . From end to end the great room in my house was put in
mourning, and lined down to the outward door. Silver sconces in
the rooms, and black, without, waxlights and scutcheons; the coffin,
velvet, black, with gilt nails and handles; the body in the with
drawing room, with all tapers and mourners and like sconces".
(Augustus Jessop, *Lives of the Norths*, Vol. III, p. 229).

[2] Hatchments.

[3] Became "a nun of the Order of St Augustine, at Paris".

[4] Married James Fermor, of Tusmore, co. Oxon, esquire, a member
of a well-known Roman Catholic family.

[5] A loose gown. "Lost, a Flowered Manto Gown of a Sable and
Gold Colour, lined with black". (*True Protestant Mercury*, No. 162,
1682, quoted in S. W. Beck's *The Draper's Dictionary*).

[6] Probably one of the Clarkes of Chisfield.

Mr Wayte a tailor, for finding materials and making a mourning coat or cloak for the tutor, and for the French servant, was paid £6 9s. and also £2 12s. for a mourning suit and coat for the testator's daughter's footboy; a sum of £7 17s. 6d. was laid out for hoods, gloves, muffs, linen, stockings, shoes, scarves, ribbons, etc. for the testator's two eldest daughters'[1] mourning; and Richard Kempton, a tailor, for making the children's servant's mourning, was paid 17s.; Crowch, a mercer in Stevenage, charging £1 10s. 7d. for the materials; and hats, shoes, gloves, cravats, etc. were purchased for Burbery himself, and for the French servant, for £2 8s., which is the concluding item concerning the actual funeral clothing of the deceased's family and servants.

In addition to all these things funeral wine was purchased of Mrs Pitches of Hitchin. It cost as much as £16 18s., and there was also a payment of £3 16s. to Mr Wilson at the Pope's Head[2] near the Royal Exchange for canary for the funeral. Thus altogether the funeral-wine took quite a high place in these disbursements.

Payments amounting to £3 6s. were made to a waggoner for carriage [to Chisfield] of several boxes, wine, cloth, and baize, and to porters at several times.

The next items were to William Bray for a lined coffin, £3 16s., and for work then done in Chisfield church about railing-in the grave, and materials, £2 1s. 10d. There was a small family-chapel in the little church, concerning which there is a payment, to the bricklayer or mason for work done about the chapel and grave, of 14s. 6d.; and one to the local blacksmith, for iron-work to support the banners in the church, 8s. 6d., these of course being the heraldic banners which had been borne at the funeral. John Hyde, a plumber, for wrapping up the coffin in lead, was paid £4 16s.; and the sexton made the grave, for which work, together with his dues, he received £4 16s.

---

[1] There was a third daughter, Elizabeth, very young at the time of her father's death. She eventually became "a nun of the monastery of St Clare at Rouen".

[2] Probably the Pope's Head in Cornhill, the best-known of the four London taverns of that sign, and then much patronized by Roman Catholics. It was here that Pepys drank his first dish of tea in 1660.

A sum of £15 was paid to Mrs George Throckmorton at Chisfield for diet, lodging, etc., for several persons resorting thither upon account of the funeral, from the testator's death till the interment, being about five weeks. This is followed by one of £14 11s. to the servants of Mr Throckmorton and others who attended and watched with the testator day and night, in sickness and after death, till the interment. The parson[1]—perforce the Protestant rector of Graveley—for burying the corpse, received a fee of £1 1s. 6d., and £2 10s. was paid as the penalty upon the statute of composition for burying the testator's corpse in linen, instead of wool, as ordered by the Act of Parliament for Burial in Woollen, which had come into force in 1667, but was not rigidly enforced until a second one had been enacted in August, 1678. Under the Act a further sum of £2 10s. was also to be given to the poor of the parish upon the Sunday next following the interment, but the payment is not noted in these disbursements.[2]

To a brazier for the use of six candlesticks which held the tapers for twenty-five days together by the corpse, at one shilling per day, Burbery paid £1 5s., and William Porter, a hackney-coachman, charged £2 15s. for the use of a coach and four horses for three days at the interment, from London to Chisfield, a distance of some thirty-three miles.

Timothy Scoto, an upholsterer, was paid for his journey and pains in hanging the rooms with mourning at Chisfield, £2 6s.; and Mrs Bowyer's bill for mansmeat and horsemeat upon the funeral occasions, amounted to £6 3s. 7d.

Finally there were certain items which Burbery had paid out of his own pocket and for which he was now reimbursed, viz. travelling charges in several journeys from Chisfield to London and back again about the funeral occasion, £5; together with £6 10s. 10d. paid for his and other servants' horsehire and other expenses in several journeys to London, Bucks, Essex, etc. upon occasion of the testator's death and funerals; and of £1 9s. 9d. in small necessary things for Misses Anne and Mary Throckmorton soon after their father's death.

[1] Philip Osbaldestone, rector from 1662 to 1697.

[2] It duly appears, however, in the Graveley parish registers, where there is this entry: 'Dec. 8th, 1680, Sʳ Francis Throckmorton, Baronet. Buried at Chisfield, and fifty shillings paid to yᵉ poor.'

All these funeral expenses therefore amounted to the large sum of £378 19s. 1d.[1] which—at least at that time—the estate could not really afford.

And what did all this pomp and circumstance come to in the end? Less than fifty years later Sir Henry Chauncy notes, under Chisfield[2]: "... And in the Chapel [in the church] did lye the Body of Sir Francis Throckmorton, of Great Coughton, in the County of Warwick, Baronet, who dyed the [7th] day of November, 1680, which Chapel is adorned with his Banner and Bannerols and the Ensigns belonging to his Degree . . . but his eldest son, Sir Robert, lately removed his Body from hence to the ancient Burying Place of his Ancestors at Coughton . . ." The church, which had already suffered badly in the early days of the Commonwealth, was now slowly becoming a ruin. It can scarcely be thought, therefore, and also considering its size, that Sir Robert had first erected the imposing marble monument in Chisfield church,[3] and that later on he had caused it to be removed to Weston church at the same time that, in filial devotion, he had his father's body brought from Chisfield to be reburied in the old church at Coughton.

In any case the monument is now at the east end of the south aisle in Weston Church.

It first of all commemorates, in Latin inscriptions, our Francis; his eldest son, Francis, who, as already noted, had died at Bruges on September 10th, 1676, aged 16, and whose heart was brought for burial at Weston; and Robert—the eldest son of the above Sir Robert—who died in his early infancy, in November, 1688. Then, beneath, are inscriptions incised much later on, commemorating Sir George Throckmorton, who died on July 27th, 1826, aged 72; and his wife, Catherine (née Stapleton), who died on January 22nd, 1839.

---

[1] The funeral in 1641 of the wealthy Earl of Bedford, had cost "£257 without the mourning". (Gladys Scott Thomson, *Life in a Noble Household*, p. 42).

[2] *Antiquities of Hertfordshire*, (1726), Vol. II, p. 125–26.

[3] "At the upper end of the south aisle is a very handsome monument of white marble, embellished with black . . ." It is faintly visible in the illustration of the interior of V.C.H., *Buckinghamshire*, Vol. IV, facing p. 501, and is approximately 14 feet in height, and 4 feet wide.

CHAPTER VII

THE WILL AND ITS REVELATION

Francis had made his last will,[1] a long one, on November 13th, 1676. At that time he describes himself as being of Great Coughton,[2] and, optimistically, of perfect health of body and mind, blessed be God therefor, but having lived to see the unhappy day of my dear son Francis Throckmorton's death. Consequently he revokes all former wills, and makes this new will, committing his soul to God that gave it, and his body to the earth from whence it was taken to be buried in what place his executors hereafter shall think fit, according to his degree and quality.

Certainly the state of his finances had greatly improved after the Restoration—for that and other reasons—and there are many bequests, which it is not necessary to follow in detail. One of them is that the yearly rents of the manor of Oversley amounting to £40, are to be paid "to my faithful servant Henry St John[3] of the Inner Temple", which seems to add support to the belief—which no research has been able definitely to prove—that Francis was of the legal

[1] P.C.C. 81 North. A photostat copy of this will has now been deposited at Birmingham Reference Library. In the course of the Chancery Proceedings complaint which follows, it is stated that Francis had also made another will, on July 11th, 1680, not long before his death.

[2] In 1678, the imaginary 'Popish Plots' led to a fresh return of recusants, and a list of fourteen names in Buckinghamshire was drawn up in connexion with the proposed 'Bill for the Removing and Disarming of Papists'. The best-known name on this list is that of Sir John Fortescue of Salden, and it is stated that "Sir Francis Throgmorton of Weston Underhill [sic] is no longer living in the county".

[3] Probably Henry St John of Farley Chamberlayne, co. Southampton, gent., who had been admitted at the Inner Temple, May 11th, 1661.

profession and at one time had chambers at the Inner Temple. There is also a bequest "to my cousin Mr Francis Leveson"—who was certainly a member of that profession—"in case he be living with me at my decease."

And now, somewhat mysteriously—for the lady's name has never appeared elsewhere in all these matters until it is now revealed—a certain Bridget Tyldesley, concerning whom much more will follow, is bequeathed £1,000; and there are, amongst others, legacies to John Crosse, of St Clement Danes, London; and to Francis's cousin, John Golding, living at Rouen.

An indenture made between Francis and Anne on the one part, and the Hon. Thomas Talbot, of Longford, co. Salop, Sir Anthony Chester, of Chicheley, co. Buckingham, baronet, Richard Reeve, of Great Coughton, esquire, and James Smith, Francis's former steward, "since deceased", on the other part, dated January 20th, 1670, is recited. It evidences that Francis, in addition to being lord of the manor of Weston, with the rectory thereof, and of the manor of Throckmorton, also owned the Warwickshire manors of Coughton, Spernal *alias* Spernhold, Sambourne, Oversley, Exhall, Wixford (Wicklesford), and Upton, near Alcester. The rents from all these manors are to be paid, during the heir's minority, "to Dame Anne, my wife", in accordance with the terms of her jointure. This is the only reference, and a very distant one at that, to Anne, who at the time of Francis's death had already for some time been living more or less apart from him and their family at Coughton Court.

The three executors, the aforesaid St John, Crosse, and Golding, are all to have mourning rings worth £10 each, and to be guardians of all the children until they are of age. For them testator makes careful provision, and he desires the guardians "to see my said children piously and virtuously educated according to their degrees and qualities in the principles of the same true Catholic faith which I do and have ever professed and followed". Francis, when making his will, was living in more spacious days than those of his father, who in his own will had been unable to make any such profession of faith as this, doubtless much as he would like to have done so.

Finally testator leaves to Robert,[1] my elder son and heir, all my household goods, plate, jewels, horses and cattle at Weston and Coughton, and £3,000 each to his children, George, Anne and Mary.

The witnesses to this will were Jasper Walker, Peter Crosse, Edward Matthews, Henry St John, Samuel Derby, James West, and John Valentine. To a codicil made on July 11th, 1680, the witnesses were Henry St John, Walter St John, and John Burbery. Probate was granted to Henry St John on May 19th, 1681.

And now what about this Bridget Tyldesley? She seemed to be well worth further documentary pursuit, and the resolve being once taken a variety of possible sources of information were explored in vain. At length the time came to examine the calendars of contemporary Chancery Proceedings at the Public Record Office. Amongst their vast number it transpired that there still exist files of documents concerning half-a-dozen suits with which Francis and his son, Robert, were—one or the other—more or less closely associated. Examination of several of them proved negative, and then came one which presented distinct possibilities, for it was no less than Throckmorton *v.* Tyldesley,[2] a suit which has certainly made possible the addition of some very interesting information, albeit all rather sad, concerning the later years of Francis and Anne, those years in which Bridget Tyldesley was destined to play a very considerable part.

The complaint in this suit is dated October 23rd, 1682— a little less than two years after the death of Francis—the complainants named being young Sir Robert, together with his brother, George, and his three sisters, Anne, Mary, and

---

[1] See p. 2. Born at Weston Underwood, January 10th, 1662. "1718. December 17th. Mr Robert Eyton tells me that Sir Robert Throgmorton is a man of about £5,000 per annum at least. This Sir Robert Throgmorton, who hath one seat at Buckland near Faringdon, Berkshire, is a Roman Catholic, and a very worthy man". (*Reliquiae Hearnianae*, Vol. II, p. 87). He died on March 8th, 1720, and was buried at Weston. At Coughton Court there is a bound volume of memoranda made by him, chiefly relating to the management of his property and to farming affairs. (Hist. MSS. Comm., 3rd Report, p. 257).

[2] C. P., Reynardson, 1682, 81/12.

Elizabeth, all infants under the age of twenty-one. Their complaint is therefore actually made through the aforesaid Henry St John, acting as guardian and next friend, and there is no evidence that their mother took any active part at all in these proceedings.

The complaint, after full reference has been made to the details of Francis's foregoing will, then comes to the cause of the whole matter, which is that legacy of £1,000 to Bridget Tyldesley, whom, not ungallantly but usefully—and the Throckmortons did it too—we will hereafter know just as Tyldesley. Concerning her, St John does not beat about the bush. He says that she was a mean servant maid and in no way related to Sir Francis or any of his family. About a year before he made his will, in November, 1676, she was "taken in to be a servant at Weston to live in the said family in the place of a laundry maid"[1]. After she had been there for some time "she did by several cunning acts and insinuations get in to be much in favour of Sir Francis, and was after some time entrusted by him with all or a good part of his cash and with the receiving of his moneys and rents . . . and with all or a great part of his jewels, old gold, plate, and other things, besides securities for moneys . . . For divers years before his death she received about £200 per annum of his moneys".

St John proceeds to suggest that Tyldesley received other rents too, which she converted to her own use, and she used "many cunning and sinister acts, ways, and means, and at last did prevail so far upon Sir Francis as to get him to put into his will such legacy as aforesaid". She has now brought a bill against Sir Robert and his brother and sisters to make them pay this legacy of £1,000.

Tyldesley, the complaint continues, had already received at least £2,500 from Sir Francis, to whom she eventually proved very ungrateful, and he had intended "to go up to London to alter his will, but before he could do so he died, leaving very little or no ready moneys by him at his death, or

---

[1] Which, of course, was not unusual at that time, and much later, in cases in which parents with many children and little means had to find situations for their daughters in respectable—but not always so—households.

out at interest on any securities except those taken in her name, which she has possessed herself of, and by reason thereof the said young children are not likely to receive their portions for many years, if at all, and can scarce have sufficient maintenance in the meantime. Yet she most unreasonably demands and insists on having the said £1,000". Finally the complainant bluntly states that Bridget had lived with Sir Francis for some thirteen years before his death.

It was now the defendant's turn, and in her answer to the complaint she doth confess that she was a servant to Lady Anne, "but not so mean of birth" as has been alleged, "she being descended from a branch of the family of Tyldesley[1] in Lancashire, a family well known both for its antiquity and loyalty, nor by Lady Anne received under so mean a character as laundry maid, nor did she make it her business to look after the service of the said Lady Anne, but was by her ladyship herself sought after and desired to serve her as her gentlewoman, to wait upon her and be with her in her chamber and sit at her own table".

Thus she lived in the family for two years, and then "some fourteen or fifteen years ago there happened such frequent and unhappy differences between Sir Francis and Lady Anne, notwithstanding all the endeavours of several friends and relations concerned in the welfare of the family and of Tyldesley herself, that she did absolutely quit her service and returned to London from whence Lady Anne had before sent for her to come as aforesaid".

About eighteen months after her return to London, Tyldesley says that Lady Anne begged her to come back and live with her, not as a servant but as a friend, "and to be accommodating and composing of the great disorders and differences which were betwixt her and Sir Francis". Upon her ladyship's great importunity Tyldesley says that she accordingly did go in the stage coach for Banbury,

[1] Sir Thomas Tyldesley, of Tyldesley, co. Lancaster, who fell at Norgrove on August 25th, 1651, fighting for the Royalist cause, had a daughter, Bridget, who eventually married Henry Blundell, nephew of Ince Blundell, esquire, and died without issue. (Edward Baines, *Lancashire*, Vol. II, p. 608, with pedigree). She is very unlikely, however, to have been identical with this Mistress Bridget.

whither Lady Anne sent her own coach, being a day's journey from Coughton, the place where she then laid, and her gentlewoman along with it, to accompany Tyldesley back to Coughton.

Upon Tyldesley's arrival at Coughton, Lady Anne received her with every mark and expression of kindness, and Tyldesley lived with her at Coughton for twelve or fifteen months, and did her best to accommodate those unhappy differences between her ladyship and her husband, and by her great industry and solicitation got a private meeting between them at Coughton at which Tyldesley was not only also present, but did so happily succeed therein, that they were perfectly reconciled before they parted, Francis presumably returning to Weston. After this Lady Anne repeatedly expressed her thanks to Tyldesley, and embraced her, on account of her true love and kindness.

However, a fresh occasion of unkindness arose, and Tyldesley took her leave, and retired to a friend's house not far distant from Coughton. Evidently on this occasion the trouble was just between Lady Anne and Tyldesley, and only a short time elapsed before her impetuous ladyship sent—two days in succession—two gentlemen, her friends, successively to persuade Tyldesley to return to Coughton. They failed, so on the third day Lady Anne came herself, and took her home with her in her coach much against her will. Tyldesley says that she stayed a little longer there, but could neither serve the Lady nor have any content herself, so she once more took her leave, and also the coach for London, where she has lived more or less ever since. She adds that she very much liked Sir Francis and Lady Anne, and their children; and also that she did receive £200 per annum from Sir Francis, but this was because she remained a friend of the family, and she returned a part of it as is well known.

As for the allegation that she had also received jewels, old gold, and plate from Sir Francis, Tyldesley answers that she received none of these things, save only one battered silver porringer and a spoon, both of the value of thirty shillings or thereabouts, which Sir Francis gave to her for her own use, nor was she ever entrusted with anything of that nature. She had heard, however, that Sir Francis had a parcel of old gold which he gave to Richard Edes, of Warwick, to buy furniture for a house. When Sir Francis made his first will, on December 22nd, 1671, St John suggested that she should have less than the £1,000, but Sir Francis said, "No, poor woman, I will never lessen her".

As to complainant's suggestion that she had for some time lived with Sir Francis, she shows no resentment but craves leave to insert two letters, being all she can find of the many she had formerly received from Lady Anne; and one from young Robert Throckmorton, during the time he was with his late father in France.

'The Lady', the answer continues, 'wrote as followeth: 'April 9, [in Eastertide, but no year is given] Dear Tyldesley, whereas of late according to the diversity of humours there hath been some mispressions no less ungrateful to me than to yourself, I thought good—the opportunity of this bearer concurring with this Paschal season of peace and soul's joy—to signify unto you that I never harboured any opinion prejudicial to your modesty, but ever thought you honest, as piety obliged me, nothing been manifest to the contrary. This I have often upon occasion declared in your behalf, and do by these presents attest unto you, so that I hope you will be so charitable to yourself, and do me that right as to banish all sinister thoughts to the contrary, and as good Christians let us bury all former disgusts in the wounds of our Blessed Saviour, our peacemaker. I do heartily wish you all happiness and, may your health and occasions be such as to come into these parts, you shall be truly welcome to her who will assuredly be, dear Tyldesley, yours in all good offices, Anne Throckmorton'.

The very next day Lady Anne wrote the second of these letters, thus:

'Dear Tyldesley, I would have you come down to me with all speed, for the world shall see that I esteem you an honest woman. Therefore do not fail, but make haste, for I am impatient till thou comest, that I may make thee happy, and redeem thy honour efficaciously'. Probably dear Tyldesley knew what her ladyship actually meant, although it was perhaps rather unfortunately expressed. The letter continues: 'Let not Mr Palgrave [an attorney] trouble himself any further, for I do not need anybody's persuasion to make it appear that I am your very good friend, Anne Throckmorton'.

Robert's aforementioned letter,[1] written to Tyldesley on June 8th [no year[2]] was as follows:

'Dear Madam, my father received yours yesterday, which troubled him so much that he hath been very ill this night. It is not only the death of Biddle[3] that afflicteth him so much, I find, but that you answered nothing about your coming over [to France], which is his and my greatest affliction, for he hath not been right since his coming over here, but I fear this will cast him quite down, because that in his melancholy fits and troubles he was used to comfort himself with the hopes of seeing you here. But now, taking your silence for a denial, I am afeared he will cast himself with melancholy into some distemper, if he receiveth no better news from you, for the despair of your not coming and Biddle's death together wholly afflict him, whereas if you gave him any hopes of your coming, I am confident he would moderate his concern for Biddle.

'As for my particular wish I hope that you will not refuse me that, for I should be extremely concerned to go to voyage without seeing you and Mistress Letrio,[4] which always had such a kindness for me. As for your coming, you may find those that know the language to come along with you and my sister. If poor Biddle is dead, my father would have John Burbery come over with you, and somebody else that understands the language.

'I hope you will consider how much ten or twelve days' journey will rejoice our whole family, and settle my father's resolutions, and render him happy that shall always be your most affectionate and humble servant, R. Throckmorton.

[1] He gives no address, but it is probable that he was writing from Rouen, and that he was apprenticed to John Golding, a ship broker there.

[2] It would seem to be 1679, the year after Titus Oates's Plot.

[3] A manservant who had been his faithful attendant.

[4] A former family governess who had taught them Italian.

'I beseech you present my service to dear Mistress Letrio. I pray you again consider the case my father is in, and the consequence of it'.

Tyldesley adds that her carriage and behaviour to Sir Francis was never other than what was suitable to his honour and quality, and fit for and becoming herself, and not in any sort contrary to the rules of virtue and modesty, and so viewed and looked upon by himself, as she believes, for he was used—when in this country—not only to write, but to send his servant on purpose to be informed of her health, she being then as she still is, a very sickly and infirm woman.

Not long since, soon after the death of Sir Francis, Tyldesley says that in the presence of Sir Robert—as he now was— she asked St John if Sir Francis had ever expressed a wish to alter his will, and he replied, "No, let all go as it is". Also, much about the same time, Sir Francis told her himself that he would never lessen her, and further that if there were any faith in man she would have her legacy paid her.

In conclusion, Tyldesley admits that Sir Francis did in his lifetime commit the care and keeping of his last will and testament to her. She very unwillingly did this service, and frequently requested Sir Francis to take it out of her hands and leave it with St John, but Sir Francis absolutely refused to do so. Several other associated documents do not produce any additional information, and there the story ends, for there is no existing record of the finding of the Court. It seems almost incredible that Sir Robert, even though he were only a young man, should have permitted himself to be the complainant in this suit, simply for the sake of his dead father's honour. He, too, must have surely remembered that foregoing letter which he himself had written to Tyldesley. Actually, one cannot help feeling that Henry St John must have inspired the whole proceeding, in the course of which an evidently base suggestion was made against the morality of the dead Sir Francis and the living, fragile Tyldesley.

How far Anne was or was not implicated in the complaint is another question, and there is no need to pursue it. She and Francis had begun their married life with much in their favour, and they were blessed with children. Gradually, however, Anne's somewhat extravagant and dilatory ways, and perhaps her card-playing for stakes the height of which may have vexed her always careful husband, began the trouble. Then incompatibility of temper, mordant jealousy and many recriminations began to play their very direful parts and, together with that state of acute melancholia into which Francis at last sank, accomplished the ultimate and hopeless separation of husband and wife, despite the fact that apparently they were both deeply religious people.

Small wonder, therefore, that Anne's name does not appear upon that great memorial in Weston church. She lived to be an old lady—nearer ninety than eighty—dying at Coughton Court in 1728, where she must have been so well-known, and there she was buried. She had spent her widowhood of almost half a century at that old house, and even before then she had sometimes lived there apart from her husband, and evidently from her young children, too.[1] Probably it was then that the house began, for the time being, to fall into that condition—'a wretched old house with a handsome gate of stone'[2]—of which Horace Walpole thus wrote in August, 1758, when describing his visit to Warwickshire.

A little less than a century previous, so it has been said without any evidence, Francis—after the Restoration—had been responsible for many improvements to the mansion, and there, in happier times, had dispensed considerable hospitality to his friends.

If the many ghosts of Coughton Court ever walk o'nights—and it is confidently said that they do—then Francis and Anne must surely be prominent in that historic and shadowy procession, although perhaps still separated from one another.

[1] At Coughton Court there is a transcript, also at present inaccessible, of a "Life of Edward Throckmorton, who died in the English College at Rome, 18th November, 1582". (Hist. MSS. Comm., 3rd Report, p. 257). The transcript "was finished at Coughton in September, 1677, at two o'clock after dinner", and it may eventually transpire that it was made by the lonely Anne.

[2] Concerning which there is a wrong tradition that it came from Evesham Abbey after its suppression in 1539, at which time Sir George Throckmorton was high-steward there.

It was indeed all a pathetic conclusion, and yet everything had seemed so happy when those Weston maidens strewed flowers before our kindly, well-intentioned young country gentleman and his radiant bride on that summer day in far-off 1659. Autumn and winter—their matrimonial autumn and winter too—were not far distant. And so the end.

Index